PROBLEMS OF EARLY CHILDHOOD

GARLAND REFERENCE LIBRARY
OF SOCIAL SCIENCE
(VOL. 129)

PROBLEMS OF EARLY CHILDHOOD
An Annotated Bibliography and Guide

Elisabeth S. Hirsch

GARLAND PUBLISHING, INC. • NEW YORK & LONDON
1983

Library of Congress Cataloging in Publication Data

Hirsch, Elisabeth S.
   Problems of early childhood.

   (Garland reference library of social science ; v. 129)
   Includes indexes.
   1. Children—Bibliography.   2. Children–Juvenile
literature—Bibliography.   3. Separation (Psychology)—
Bibliography.   4. Separation (Psychology)—Juvenile
literature—Bibliography.   5. Socialization—Bibliography.
6. Socialization—Juvenile literature—Bibliography.
I. Title. II. Series.
Z5814.C5H57 1983 [HQ767.9] 016.3053'2   82-49031
ISBN 0-8240-9216-3

Cover design by Laurence Walczak

Printed on acid-free, 250-year-life paper
Manufactured in the United States of America

CONTENTS

v

ACKNOWLEDGMENTS

My grateful acknowledgments are due first and foremost to my husband Julius E. Hirsch, who believed in me, supported me both spiritually and with his two typing fingers. To say I could not have finished this book without him is not telling the whole truth. I would never have started it!

My friend Bertha Campbell was more than helpful in obtaining bibliographic information.

Dr. Jean Mandelbaum was an editor extraordinaire for the beginning essays and helped me to overcome my "writer's block."

Susan Hirsch, daughter and colleague, provided suggestions that were always pertinent.

Anne Goldstein, with magic fingers and knowledge of form, pulled it all together.

Thank you.

INTRODUCTION

If I were asked as the ancient sage, Hillel was: "Can you summarize this book while standing on one foot?" I would reply: "The problems of childhood result from being a child." Children are helpless and dependent for many years. Experiences involving separation, entering school, moving, hospitalization, the death of beloved persons, divorce, single parents, mothers going to work, leave them with fears of abandonment and loss. Having to share parents with a sibling can also cause feelings of abandonment and deprivation. Another condition of childhood that can become problematic has to do with the child's gradual entry into society—socialization creates discipline problems; learning to interact with peers can result in difficulties in social relationships.

This sums up nine sections of this book. The tenth one— Strong Feelings—deals less with cause and effect than with the need to handle the emotional side of one's nature. Oddly, current literature seems to neglect this topic, which received overwhelming attention in the 50s. Are we becoming uncomfortable— the way our parents and grandparents used to be—at the thought that young children do have strong feelings? Or have our concerns shifted from the child and his needs to the adult and his expectations, as exemplified by the prevalent concern about early attainment of skills and the emphasis on behavior modification?

This book examines literature dealing with most of the problems young children, their parents, and their teachers face. Topics are introduced by bibliographic essays followed by annotated listings subdivided into Books and Pamphlets for Adults, Studies and Articles, and Books for Children. Studies and Articles include single chapters in books as well as documents available from Educational Resources Information Center (ERIC), a database containing material on education.

Books for children can be used effectively in the home as well as in the classroom. Children are often relieved when they find that their experiences and feelings are shared by others. The stories also open the door to communication between adults and children. The bibliographies include a number of discussions on ways to use such books with children. See, for instance, selections 3, 28, 29, 141, 160, 177, 243, 244, 310, 357, 469, 701, 703, 927, 999, 1000. Books that are out of print are listed as they are generally available in libraries. We did not find any books for children dealing specifically with discipline, except for those of the "moralizing" kind. Most educators and psychologists do not recommend these books. Discipline, it seems, while of major concern to parents and teachers, cannot be visualized by children under seven as an "issue" or "crisis" where identifying with others in similar situations can bring insight and comfort. The chapter on "Discipline" differs in its format from other chapters in another respect. Books and Pamphlets for parents are listed separately from those for teachers, since discipline at home presents problems different from those in the classroom.

A major area of concern has been omitted from this volume. Handicapping conditions and the literature dealing with them are so varied and profuse that this volume cannot do the subject justice and, therefore, they are not included.

It is our hope that this book will assist those who wish to help children cope with the common problems of being a child in contemporary society.

PROBLEMS OF EARLY CHILDHOOD

SEPARATION EXPERIENCES

Nestlings, chirping as they await their mother's return with a juicy worm, express not only their hunger, I am sure. They must be worried that she may never return at all.

Human children remain helpless and dependent much longer than baby birds. They do not achieve independence for many years. In fact, we have now learned that they are not even sure of their selfhood when they are very young. The research of Margaret Mahler (33, 37) teaches us that for approximately the first five months of his life a baby is not sure where he ends and where his mother* begins. During this phase, which Dr. Mahler calls the *symbiotic period*, babies can accept any loving caretaker without undue upset.

Only after this first period does the process of "hatching" begin and the world "other than mother" enter the infant's consciousness. The infant begins to emerge from oneness by recognizing his mother as a separate person. He plays with her face and other features and with his own, recognizing their separateness. Wariness of others, "stranger anxiety," has been found to crop up during this stage, which seems to be a time of special vulnerability, should separation from the mother occur during this period.

*The word "mother" does not have to be restricted to the biological mother, as used in these pages. It does have to be, however, *one* "significant adult," male or female, who is a stable presence while the child matures. For stylistic reasons the pronouns "she" and "her" are used for the mothering adult, while "he" and "him" are used for children of either sex.

1

After this period of "differentiation" comes—around nine months—the stage of "practicing," thus named because it is at this time that the infant practices his newly acquired motor skills. The baby begins to crawl and to stand up. He moves literally away from his mother. This is a time of exploring the environment and the people in it. As he ventures further from his mother he returns to her occasionally for emotional refueling by re-establishing physical contact with her. Toddlers of this stage (9-18 months) seem to have a love affair with the world. Mahler says that the junior toddler taking his first steps feels that the world is his oyster! This is the time when the child as an individual emerges. The independence of the junior toddler is misleading, however. Children were observed withdrawing into themselves and losing interest in their surroundings if their mothers became unavailable. They would burst into tears if approached by a friendly adult. Mahler concluded that the toddler concentrated on focusing his attention on the memory of his mother.

At about a year and a half the period of elation ceases. The senior toddler, having become increasingly aware of his separateness and helplessness, vents his frustration in negativism. The "no" stage is hard on mothers, who feel rejected and powerless. Children seem to dart away on one hand and to be clinging on the other. The clinging behavior indicates the continuing separation anxiety of the toddler who is still not quite able to maintain a mental image of his mother. The senior toddler begins to establish firm relationships with familiar, nonthreatening adults.

The final phase of separation-individuation begins at approximately two years. This is the period of consolidation of individuality. The child is able to function for increasingly long intervals without his mother's presence. His mental image of his mother is now firm. He can carry her around in his mind. He develops speech and has an increasing ability to comprehend reality. Sense of time develops at this age (although time for little children goes much, much more slowly than for adults) and children are finally able to comprehend that mother will return in time.

Mahler's explicit description of psychological maturation during the early years is not the only basis of knowledge that we have of the meaning of separation to the young child. John Bowlby (30, 31, 68, 69, 70) feels that the child's need for closeness to his mother is the central theme of his life. He found that children's response to separation, such as hospitalization, was similar to adult mourning, i.e., that it proceeded from protest to despair to denial. The Robertsons (73) who cooperated with Bowlby on the hospitalization studies, found that while a mourning-like response can occur it is not unavoidable. Children cared for by a trusted and reliable adult in their own home or even in foster care did not show symptoms of mourning.

Winnicott (43) describes the substitutes young children find, that help them to tolerate the mother's absence through the use of a "transitional object." The much beloved teddy bear or dirty old blanket is known to all of us and has even entered present-day mythology as the blanket carried by Linus of the *Peanuts* cartoons.

Children's adaptation to separation will depend on many factors. Age and a firm foundation of trust in the world are of prime importance. One and a half to two years seems a particularly vulnerable age period. Temperamental differences (42), family stability or instability (66, 75), previous experiences (75) all play their role. However, even when children have reached the point where their mothers' image is firmly rooted in their consciousness, leaving an environment and people they know and trust can be frightening and traumatic. Getting accustomed to a strange place and learning to trust strangers can be accomplished, but should be facilitated with patience and wisdom.

Short separations, well timed and well handled, can be a growth promoting experience. Curry and Tittnich (50) provide sound guidelines for assessing the readiness of children to enter school.

Speers et al. (61) offer a detailed description of children's reactions to entering the strange new world of preschool. Such reactions include a temporary regression (becoming more baby-ish, a response common under all sorts of situations of stress) and even a shortened recapitulation of earlier stages of development. Phased adjustment, where the mother spends gradually decreasing lengths of time in school, is urged by Speers and many others (50, 51, 61). As children learn to trust their teachers, become acquainted with the new environment and their class-mates they also realize that they have accomplished a feat, that they have overcome a challenge. Anyone witnessing such a process will not fail to remark on the visible "blossoming" of such a child.

Adjustment to school is complicated by the ambivalent feelings of parents (10, 13, 54). On the one hand it is hard to hand your child over to strangers, no matter how nice they seem. On the other hand, mothers usually look forward to some free time they can call their own. If they plan to go back to work, their impatience will be even more increased—so will their possible sense of guilt. Teachers should accept the respon-sibility of helping the parent as well as the child. Mothers need to be helped in deciding *when* and *how* to leave. On the other hand, children can feel devastated—totally deserted—if their parents fail to show up in time to pick them up. The slow-ticking clock of early childhood slows to a snail's pace at such times. Five minutes can seem like an eternity.

There are many other kinds of separation that are hard on children. Moving to a new home is a fairly common occurrence. Kliman (20) feels that the familiar environment itself may play a role similar to a "transitional object." Part of the reason moving seems to be so hard on little children is that adults are busy, preoccupied and probably anxious themselves. Whether the young child is underfoot, only to be shoved away, or is "farmed out" somewhere until the worst is over, he senses the turmoil and feels the loss. Favorite objects and pets become terribly important symbols of permanence at such times and should not be discarded with other old junk.

The bibliography in this section contains many books written for children about the experience of moving (78-96). Reading and discussing such stories before and after the move will help sharing of feelings and will effectively reduce anxieties.

The same can be said about the other books for children listed in the bibliography. Children seem to derive genuine solace from books that describe experiences and feelings similar to their own.

The bibliography contains a rich selection on entering school (97-112) and has material on many other kinds of separation, such as parting from beloved people, sleeping away from home, being lost, losing a pet, going to camp, and so forth (113-140). In fact, adults may find that these children's books will help them to enter the world of children's thoughts and feelings as well.

BIBLIOGRAPHY

BOOKS AND PAMPHLETS FOR ADULTS

Moving

1. Cohen, Monroe D., ed. *When Children Move from School to School*. Washington, D.C.: Association for Childhood Education International, 1972.

   Deals with school adjustment and family adjustment problems associated with moving. It also has a brief section on migrant children.
2. Coles, Robert. *Uprooted Children: The Early Life of Migrant Farm Workers*. Pittsburgh, Pa.: University of Pittsburgh Press, 1970.

   An account of the lives of migrant children who face the continuing crises of moving and poverty throughout their childhoods.
3. Fassler, Joan. *Helping Children Cope: Mastering Stress Through Books and Stories*. New York: Free Press, 1978.

   A collection of articles that discuss both parents' and the school's part in helping children.
4. Kliman, Gilbert. *Psychological Emergencies of Childhood*. New York: Grune & Stratton, 1968.

   Discusses moving from the point of view of the young child for whom his environment may play a role similar to the one of a "transitional object."
5. McCarthy, Jan. "Coping with a New Environment." In

Helping Children Cope with Change, edited by Sandra M. Long and Barbara Batchelor, pp. 21–25. Terre Haute, Ind.: Indiana Association for the Education of Young Children, 1979.

Discusses various separations such as moving, hospitalization, and entering school and gives some helpful suggestions.

6. Murphy, Lois Barkley and collaborators. *The Widening World of Childhood: Paths Toward Mastery.* New York: Basic Books, 1962.

Illustrates and discusses the feeling about moving of two children who have been observed from infancy.

7. Murphy, Lois B., and Leeper, Ethel M. *Preparing for Change.* DHEW Publication OCD 73-1028. Washington, D.C.: U.S. Department of Health, Education, and Welfare, 1973.

Discusses ways to help children over changes and separations connected with moving.

8. Sutton, Elizabeth. *Knowing and Teaching the Migrant Child.* Washington D.C. National Education Association of the United States, 1960.

Extensive descriptions of the life of migrant children and the problems they encounter. Provides suggestions for teachers on meeting and solving these problems.

Entering School

9. Beyer, Evelyn. *Teaching Young Children.* Indianapolis, Ind.: Bobbs-Merrill, 1968.

Contains a sensitive and helpful section on school adjustments.

10. Blake, Elizabeth. *Hello and Goodbye.* New York: Child Study Association, 1965.

A play for parents about learning to love and let go. Raises issues around parents' feelings. Useful as a discuscussion starter.

11. Cohen, Dorothy, and Rudolf, Marguerita. *Kindergarten and Early Schooling.* Englewood Cliffs, N.J.: Prentice-Hall, 1977.

Gives helpful suggestions to teachers on easing the first days of school.

12. Danoff, Judith; Breitbart, Vicky; and Barr, Elinor. *Open for Children: For Those Interested in Early Childhood Education.* New York: McGraw-Hill, 1977.

    Contains specific and helpful suggestions to help children to start school.

13. Einbinder, Sandra S. "School Is One Step in Letting Go: A Pamphlet to Prepare Parents on How to Separate." M.Sc. Thesis, Bank Street College of Education, 1977.

    Describes the ambivalent feelings of parents who enter their child in a preschool.

14. Fassler, Joan.*Helping Children Cope: Mastering Stress Through Books and Stories.* New York: Free Press, 1978.

    Presents the use of children's literature as a help in coping with stressful experiences. The chapter on entering school contains a review of children's books and a bibliography for adults.

15. Friedman, D. L. *Education Handbook for Black Families.* Garden City, N.Y.: Anchor/Doubleday, 1980.

    Helpful chapter on helping children to adjust to child care including a checklist of helpful suggestions.

16. Freud, Anna. *Normality and Pathology in Childhood: Assessment of Development.* New York: International Universities Press, 1965.

    Develops a scheme of normal growth along "developmental lines." Considers children ready for preschool when they have achieved "object constancy," i.e., they can realize that their mother's departure is not a total loss.

17. Hendrick, Joanne. *The Whole Children: New Trends in Early Education.* 2d ed. St. Louis, Mo.: The C. V. Mosby Company, 1980.

    Discusses adjustment to school and the difficult situation that occurs when children are picked up late.

18. Janis, Marjorie Graham. *A Two-Year-Old Goes to Nursery School.* London: Tavistock Publications, 1964.

    Detailed study and description of the eventual adjustment to nursery school, moving from inordinate defenses through delayed reaction and separation anxiety to a loosening of the infantile tie in a period lasting six months. Concludes that separation anxiety will be minimized if the child becomes accustomed to the place and the person (teacher) in the presence of the mother.

19. Kellerman, Jonathan. *Helping the Fearful Child: A Guide to Everyday and Problem Anxieties*. New York: W. W. Norton, 1981.

Helpful answers to problems of parents faced with children's fears and anxieties. Provides a clear distinction between "normal" fears and those that indicate a need for professional help.

20. Kliman, Gilbert. *Psychological Emergencies of Childhood*. New York: Grune & Stratton, 1968.

See under *Moving* (5).

21. McCarthy, Jan. "Coping with a New Environment." In *Helping Children Cope with Change*, Edited by Sandra M. Long and Barbara Batchelor, pp. 21–25. Terre Haute, Ind.: Indiana Association for the Education of Young Children, 1979.

See under *Moving* (6).

22. Murphy, Lois Barclay and collaborators. *The Widening World of Childhood: Paths Toward Mastery*. New York: Basic Books, 1962.

Includes a detailed description of the process of getting used to preschool by a child who had been observed from infancy.

23. ———, and Leeper, Ethel M. *Preparing for Change*. DHEW Publication OCD 73-1028. Washington, D.C.: U.S. Department of Health, Education, and Welfare, 1973.

Discusses the various aspects of starting school. Also includes such "repeat experiences" as Monday mornings and returning after an absence.

24. Provence, Sally; Naylor, Audrey, A.; and Patterson, June. *The Challenge of Daycare*. New Haven: Yale University Press, 1977.

Chapter on separation discusses adjustment for child and parents and has some practical suggestions about ways to lessen stress. The discussion centers on children two years old and younger.

25. Read, Katherine, and Patterson, June. *The Nursery School and Kindergarten: Human Relationships and Learning.* 7th ed. New York: Holt, Rinehart, & Winston, 1980.

Detailed discussion of the adjustment process and the teacher's role.

26. Ryan, Bernard. *How to Help Your Child Start School: A Practical Guide for Parents and Teachers of Four to Six Year Olds.* New York: G. P. Putman, 1980.

Helpful not only in helping children to begin school but also in answering many questions parents may have about preschool.

27. Warren, Rita M. *Caring: Supporting Children's Growth.* Washington, D.C.: National Association for the Education of Young Children, 1977.

Discusses the feelings of children and adults in connection with school adjustment. Describes children's misunderstandings and gives suggestions on helping children to achieve successful mastery.

Various Separations

28. Bernstein, Joanne. *Books to Help Children Cope with Separation and Loss.* New York: R. R. Bowker, 1977.

29. ———. *Helping Children Cope with Death and Separation: Resources for Teachers.* Urbana, Ill.: University of Illinois, 1976.

These bibliographies are a treasury of resources of children's books, adult movies, and annotated references on research.

30. Bowlby, John. *Attachment and Loss. Volume 1. Attachment.* New York: Basic Books, 1973.

Important references contributed by a man who pioneered studies on separation and young children. The work about young children in hospitals is particularly eloquent.

31. ———. *Attachment and Loss. Volume 2. Separation: Anxiety and Anger.* New York: Basic Books, 1973.

Examines the child's behavior and emotional responses to separation from the mother. The author believes that defense against the threat of loss affects the total personality of the child.

32. Dunn, Judy. *Distress and Comfort*. Cambridge, Mass.: Harvard University Press, 1977.

    Examines the distress of young children at separation as a result of losing all familiar persons and places.

33. Edward, Joyce; Ruskin, Nathene; and Turini, Patsy. *Separation-Individuation: Theory and Application*. New York: Gardner Press, 1981.

    Presents Mahler's theory of separation-individuation with illustrative case studies.

34. Fassler, Joan. *Helping Children Cope: Mastering Stress Through Books and Stories*. New York: The Free Press, 1978.

    Annotated reference guide to children's books dealing with various stress situations. Chapter on separation deals with a variety of separations.

35. Ginott, Haim G. *Between Parent and Child: New Solutions to Old Problems*. New York: Macmillan, 1965.

    Offers many concrete suggestions that will help parents to determine their children's feelings and offers appropriate ways to respond.

36. Long, Sandra M., and Batchelor, Barbara, eds. *When There Is a Crisis: Helping Children Cope with Change*. Terre Haute, Ind.: Indiana Association for the Education of Young Children, 1979.

    Discusses various crises and offers helpful advice for parents and teachers.

37. Mahler, Margaret S.; Pine, Fred; and Bergman, Anni. *The Psychological Birth of the Human Infant: Symbiosis and Individuation*. New York: Basic Books, 1975.

    Presents separation and individuation as complementary developmental processes as the child gradually separates from the fusion with his mother during the ages of five months and three years, by moving from autism through symbiosis to object constancy, where he can retain the inner representation of his mother.

38. McCarthy, Jan. "Coping with a New Environment." In *Helping Children Cope with Change*, edited by Sandra M. Long and Barbara Batchelor, pp. 21–25. Terre Haute,

Ind.: Indiana Association for the Education of Young
Children, 1979.

See under *Moving*. (6).

39. Murphy, Lois B., and Leeper, Ethel M. *Preparing for Change.*
DHEW Publication OCD 73-1028. Washington, D.C.:
U.S. Department of Health, Education, and Welfare
1973.

Discusses ways to help children over changes and
separations of many kinds, such as starting school, teacher
absence, new babies, moving, hospitalization, and getting
shots, changes in schedule, transitions, returning to school
after absence, and separation from parents due to illness,
death, imprisonment, or divorce.

40. Nieburg, Herbert, and Fischer, Arlene. *Pet Loss: A Thoughtful
Guide for Adults and Children.* New York: Harper & Row,
1982.

Discusses feelings of pet owners (adults and children)
connected with separation, death, and losing a pet.

41. Rice, Elizabeth Prince; Ekdahl, Miriam C.; and Miller, Leo.
Children of Mentally Ill Parents: Problems in Child Care. New
York: Behavioral Publications, 1971.

The emotional reaction of children when their parents
are hospitalized in mental institutions is often severe. This
book recounts a study of such youngsters. It also contains
a comparative study of children whose parents were hospitalized for tuberculosis.

42. Smardo, Frances, A. "How Do We Help Children Cope?"
Children Education 58 (1981):40–45.

Reviews research on the psychological and emotional
effects of geographic mobility upon children. Suggestions
are given about how to help children cope with moving.

43. Thomas, Alexander, and Chess, Stella. *Temperament and Behavior Disorders in Children.* New York: New York University Press, 1969.

Considers the variety of modes of adaptation to new
situations a temperamental difference.

Studies and Articles

Moving

44. Winnicott, Donald. W. *The Maturational Process and the Facilitating Environment: Studies in the Theory of Emotional Development.* New York: International University Press, 1974.

    Contains a collection of Winnicott's papers that explore maturation and the need for dependence in the young child.

Entering School

45. Adams, Roderick E., Jr., and Passman, Richard H. "The Effects of Preparing Two-Year-Olds for Brief Separation from Their Mothers." *Child Development* 52 (1981): 1068–1070.

    Studies effects of various strategies used by mothers to prepare a two-year-old child to be left with a stranger. Children given brief preparations remained with the stranger longer and played more with toys.

46. Anderson, Luleen S. "When the Child Begins School." *Children Today* 5 (July/August 1976): 16–19.

    Practical, no-nonsense article that discusses beginning kindergarten and/or first grade.

47. Blanchard, Marie, and Main, Mary. "Avoidance of the Attachment Figure and Social-Emotional Attachment in Day Care Infants." *Developmental Psychology* 15 (1979): 445–446.

    Found that children who had spent a year in substitute care showed less avoidance behavior than cited by Blehar (566) and higher social-emotional adjustment, implying that "adjustment" of infants to substitute care may be more rapid than previously thought.

48. Bowlby, John. "Security and Anxiety." In *The Formative Years: How Children Become Members of Their Society*, edited by David Edge, pp. 19–27. New York: Schocken Books, 1972.

    Considers the young child's need for security imparted by his mother; a basic drive, important for survival.

49. Butler, Annie. L. "Tender Topics: Children and Crises." ERIC Document Reproduction Service, ED 147 019, 1977.

Describes children's feelings about and reactions to school phobias. Age differences in reactions to these crises and other separations are also discussed in terms of general cognitive development and developmental stages. Suggests that adults can help children cope with crisis situations by providing accurate information, by encouraging the expression of feelings and by managing their own feelings and attitudes toward these same events. Ways in which outside supportive services, teachers, initial family relationships and family life education can affect the child's responses to a crisis situation are also described.

50. Curry, Nancy E., and Tittnich, Ethel M. "Ready or Not Here We Come: The Dilemma of School Readiness." ERIC Document Reproduction Service, ED 168 729, 1980.

Provides guidelines for assessing school readiness (preschool and elementary) and discusses children's coping styles, the roles of parents and teachers and the feelings of parents.

51. Furman, Robert A. "Experiences in Nursery School Consultation." *Young Children* 22 (1966):84–95.

Comprehensive review of the challenges and rewards of successfully managed separation as a step toward more mature functioning.

52. Garber, Howard L. "Bridging the Gap from Preschool to School for the Disadvantaged Child." *School Psychology Digest* 8 (1979): 303–310.

Discusses school readiness of disadvantaged children. Sees the school psychologist's role in early screening and in fostering parent–school cooperation as crucial.

53. Gross, Dorothy W. "On Separation and School Entrance." *Childhood Education* 46 (1970):250–253.

Argues that a well-handled separation can strengthen the child and offers a number of suggestions.

54. Hock, Ellen. "Child's School Entry: A Stressful Event in the Lives of Fathers." *Family Relations* 29 (1980):467–472.

Finds that most fathers experience some anxiety related to their children entering school.

55. Kessler, Jane W.: Ablon, Gridth; and Smith, Edith. "Separation Reactions in Young, Mildly Retarded Children." *Children* 16 (1969):2-7.

Suggests that successfully handled separation frees individuals to benefit from the program, to learn skills, and to establish a sense of identity that will allow them to be less dependent.

56. McCarthy, Jan. "Coping with a New Environment." In *When There Is a Crisis*, edited by Sandra M. Long and Barbara Batchelor, pp. 21-25. Terre Haute, Ind.: The Indiana Association for the Education of Young Children, 1979.

Emphasizes the uniqueness of each child. Urges preparatory exploration and lists a number of contingencies that may complicate adjustments.

57. Ovitt, Jean M. "What About the School Bus?" *Young Children* 25 (1970):293-296.

Riding the school bus can be educationally enriching. It can also be outright dangerous. This article gives many suggestions.

58. Roopnarine, Jaipaul L., and Lamb, Michael E. "The Effects of Day Care on Attachment and Exploratory Behavior in a Strange Situation." *Merrill-Palmer Quarterly* 24 (1979):85-95.

Found that while three-year-olds about to enter day care were more anxious than home-care children, the differences disappeared three months later.

59. Schwarz, J. Conrad, and Wynn, Ruth. "The Effects of Mothers' Presence and Previsits on Children's Emotional Reaction to Starting Nursery School." *Child Development* 42 (1971):871-88.

Previsiting or the mother's staying for part of the first class session was found less facilitating of separation than prior nursery school experience.

60. Schwarz, J. Conrad; Krolick, George; and Strickland, Robert G. "Effects of Early Day Care Experience on Attachment to a New Environment." *American Journal of Orthopsychiatry* 43 (1973): 340-346.

Found that children with previous day care experience as toddlers showed more positive affect, less tension, and more social interaction than those attending day care for the first time when they entered the center in the company of familiar peers. However, they were rated less cooperative, more verbally aggressive, more active, and less tolerant of frustration five months later.

61. Speers, Rex W.; MacFarland, Margaret B.; Armand, Saratt; and Curry, Nancy E. "Recapitulation of Separation-Individuation Processes When the Normal Three Year Old Enters Nursery School." In *Separation-Individuation: Essays in Honor of Margaret S. Mahler*, edited by John B. McDevitt and Calvin F. Settlage, pp. 297–321. New York: International Universities Press, 1971.

Describes the temporary regression normal children go through on entering preschool and urges phased adjustment, with the mother spending gradually decreasing time in school until the child has become accustomed to the new environment. Gives criteria that will help parents and teachers to observe children and to determine when they are ready to separate.

62. Spock, Benjamin. "When Children Are Afraid to Start School." *Redbook Magazine*, August 1975. Reprinted in *Readings in Early Childhood Education 77/78*. edited by Judy Spitler McKee, pp. 145–146. Guilford, Conn.: Dushkin Publishing Group, 1977.

Suggests that reluctance to start school depends on age of child, parental expectations and adult-child relations. Offers advice for parents.

63. Yarrow, Leon J. "Separation from Parents During Early Childhood."

See under *Various Separations* (76).

Various Separations

64. Adams, Roderick E., and Passman, Richard H. "The Effects of Preparing Two-Year-Olds for Brief Separations from Their Mothers." *Child Development* 52 (1981):1068–1070.

Found that children given brief preparations could tolerate the absence of their mothers longer than those given repetitious preparations. Children were responsive to non-verbal cues.

65. Ainsworth, Mary D. Salter. "Social Development in the First Year of Life: Maternal Influences on Infant-Mother Attachment." In *Developments in Psychiatric Research Viewpoints in Review: Essays Based on Sir Geoffrey Vickers' Lectures of the Mental Health Trust and Research Fund*, edited by J. M. Tanner. London: Hodder, 1977.

Proposes that attachment behavior of infants is a genetic trait and that babies out of contact with their mothers have a built-in command to cry.

66. Bee, Helen L. "The Effect of Maternal Employment on the Development of the Child." In *Social Issues in Development Psychology*, edited by Helen L. Bee, pp. 97-106. New York: Harper & Row, 1974.

Contends that the crucial factor in children's development is the stability of the family, not the constant presence of the mother.

67. Boniface, David, and Graham, Philip. "The Three-Year-Old and His Attachment to a Special Soft Object." *Journal of Child Psychology and Psychiatry and Allied Disciplines* 20 (1979):217-224.

Mothers of 702 three year olds were asked about the use by their children of a special soft object in situations or distress and at bedtime. Object usage was then related to the children's levels of independence.

68. Bowlby, John. "Grief and Mourning in Infancy and Early Childhood." In *Psychoanalytic Study of the Child*, pp. 9-52. New York: International Universities Press, 1960.

69. ———. "Process of Mourning." *International Journal of Psychoanalysis* 42 (1961):317-340.

70. ———, and Parks, C. Murray. "Separation and Loss." In *International Yearbook for Child Psychiatry and Allied Disciplines*. Vol. 1: *The Child and His Family*, edited by E. James Anthony and Cyrille Koupernik, pp. 197-216. New York: John Wiley & Sons, 1970.

Considers young children's reactions on separation from their mothers identical to that of adult mourning.

71. Butler, Annie L. "Tender Topics: Children and Crises."
    ERIC Document Reproduction Service, ED 196 573,
    1977.

    Discusses children's responses to stressful events, de-
    scribes children's feelings about and reaction to parent
    imprisonment. Age differences in reactions to these crises
    and other separations are also discussed in terms of general
    cognitive development and developmental stages. Suggests
    that adults can help children cope with crisis situations
    by providing accurate information, by encouraging the
    expression of feelings and by managing their own feelings
    and attitudes toward these events. Ways in which outside
    supportive services, teachers, initial family relationships,
    and family life education can affect the child's responses to
    a crisis situation are also described.

72. Pine, Fred. "On the Separation Process: Universal Trends
    and Individual Differences." In *Separation-Individuation:
    Essays in Honor of Margaret S. Mahler*, edited by John B.
    McDevitt and Calvin F. Settlage, pp. 113–130. New
    York: International Universities Press, 1971.

    Follows the development of the child to separate from
    its mother from dependency to self-reliance.

73. Robertson, James, and Robertson, Joyce. "Young Children
    in Brief Separation: A Fresh Look." In *Psychoanalytic
    Study of the Child*, vol. 26, pp. 264–315. New York: Quad-
    rangle Books, 1971.

    In order to investigate whether the mourning behavior
    of children as described by Bowlby (68, 69, 70) was due to
    separation or the total ecology, the authors investigated
    children who, though separated from their parents, were
    cared for by one trusted person at their home or in foster
    care. They found that these children did not evidence
    protest, despair, and denial.

74. Rosencrantz, Louise, and Joshua, Virdia. "Children of In-
    carcerated Parents: A Hidden Population." *Children Today*
    11 (1982):2–6.

    Describes *MATCH* (Mothers And Their Children) pro-
    gram at the Federal Correctional Institution, Pleasanton,
    California, which attempts to strengthen family ties and

provide parenting experience to mothers in order to assist them in resuming their parental responsibilities.

75. Rutter, Michael, "Separation Experiences: A New Look at an Old Topic." *The Journal of Pediatrics* 95 (1980): 147–154.

   Pleads for a more differentiated look at separations, considering children's age, temperament, and previous experiences. Some separations alter circumstances for the better. Mothers not working, warring parents refraining from divorce may neglect children's needs for familial harmony. Some separations indicate psychiatric risk, however.

76. Yarrow, Leon J. "Separation from Parents During Early Childhood." In *Review of Child Development Research*, vol. 1, edited by Martin L. Hoffman and Lois Wladis Hoffman, pp. 89–136. New York: Russell Sage Foundation, 1969.

   Summary of research analyzing factors that affect children's reactions to various separations from parents, i.e., day care, institutionalization, multiple mothering, hospitalization, maternal employment, and father separation.

77. Ziegler, Patricia, and McCord, Gretchen. "Growth Through Separation: Planning for School-Leaving." ERIC Documentation Reproduction Service, ED 196 573, 1980.

   Discusses long- and short-range activities for helping children deal with separation from preschool when they are ready for kindergarten.

Books for Children

Moving to a New Neighborhood

78. Baldwin, Anne Norris. *A Friend in the Park*. New York: Four Winds, 1973.

   Eric and his mother have moved to Paris. The book depicts Eric's feelings of being left out because he does not know French. Eventually it is Eric who helps a new Portuguese girl.

79. Belpre, Pura. *Santiago*. New York: Frederick Warner, 1969.

   Describes the feelings of a boy who has recently moved from Puerto Rico to the United States.

80. Binzen, Bill. *Carmen.* New York: Coward, 1969.
    Depicts the frustrations of a newly arrived Puerto Rican
    girl, who eventually finds a friend.
81. Brown, Myra. *Pip Moves Away.* San Carlos, Calif.: Golden
    Gate Junior Books, 1967.
    Describes a young boy's confusion on moving day and
    his fear of being left behind.
82. Cohen, Miriam. *Will I Have a Friend?* New York: Collier, 1967.
    Shows the experiences of a young child entering pre-
    school in a new neighborhood.
83. Craig, Jean. *The New Boy on the Sidewalk.* New York: W. W.
    Norton, 1967.
    A boy who has recently moved to a new neighborhood
    makes a friend.
84. Hickman, Martha Whitmore. *I'm Moving.* Nashville: Abing-
    don, 1974.
    Shows how a young boy copes with moving by focusing
    on the things that will go along with him.
85. Hughes, Shirley. *Moving Molly.* Englewood Cliffs, N.J.:
    Prentice-Hall, 1978.
    Portrays the period of adjustment following a move
    from city to country.
86. Jones, Penelope. *I'm Not Moving!* Scarsdale, N.Y.: Bradbury,
    1980.
    Emmy finds understanding adults who help her work
    out her angry feelings about moving.
87. Kantrowitz, Mildred. *Goodbye Kitchen.* New York: Parents
    Magazine Press, 1972.
    Emily faces the loss of her friend who moves away.
88. Lystad, Mary. *That New Boy.* New York: Crown, 1973.
    George is unable to approach a newcomer and covers
    up his shyness by disdain.
89. Prather, Ray. *New Neighbors.* New York: McGraw-Hill, 1975.
    A little boy feels lonely and rejected when his family
    moves into a new neighborhood.
90. Robinson, Charles. *New Kid in Town.* New York: Atheneum,
    1975.
    A new arrival is victimized by a bully but is able to
    assert himself.

91. Rogers, Fred. *Mister Rogers Talks About . . .* New York: Platt & Munk, 1974.

Shows preparations prior to moving, such as fantasy play and discusses ways of not losing contact with old friends and places.

92. Schlein, Miriam. *My House.* Chicago: Albert Whitman, 1971.

Conveys the feelings a family's experiences as a house becomes their home.

93. Schulman, Janet. *The Big Hello.* New York: Greenwillow, 1976.

Depicts a young girl's cross-country move.

94. Tobias, Tobi. *Moving Day.* New York: Alfred A. Knopf, 1976.

Describes the confusion of moving, the strangeness of the new house and the final settling in, as experienced by a little girl.

95. Zolotov, Charlotte. *The Three Funny Friends.* New York: Harper & Row, 1961.

A little girl, who has moved recently, finds that she can give up her three imaginary friends when she becomes friendly with the boy next door.

96. ———. *Janey.* New York: Harper & Row, 1973.

A young girl faces her feelings of loss as she remembers her friend, who has moved away.

Entering School

97. Alexander, Martha. *Sabrina.* New York: Dial Press, 1971.

Sabrina feels self-conscious about her unusual name and decides to run away from home.

98. Amoss, Berthe. *The Very Worst Thing.* New York: Parents Magazine, 1972.

Depicts the feelings of a boy who enters a kindergarten in mid-term.

99. Barkin, Carol, and James, Elizabeth. *I'd Rather Stay Home.* Milwaukee, Wisc.: Raintree Publications, 1975.

Written in first person, it presents the feelings of Jimmy entering kindergarten.

100. Blue, Rose. *I Am Here: Yo Esto Aqui.* New York: Franklin
     Watts, 1971.
     A little Puerto Rican girl is aided in her adjustment to a
     new school, a new country, and a new language by a
     warm, supportive assistant teacher, who speaks Spanish.
101. Breinberg, Petronella. *Shawn Goes to School.* New York:
     Thomas Y. Crowell, 1973.
     Describes the support Shawn received from his family
     and the teacher when he entered nursery school.
102. Cohen, Miriam. *Will I Have a Friend?* New York: Collier,
     1967.
     Shows the experience of a young child entering pre-
     school in a new neighborhood.
103. Hurd, Edith. T. *Come with Me to Nursery School.* New York:
     Coward, 1970.
     Illustrated with photographs, it shows a nursery school
     as seen by a child.
104. Kantrowitz, Mildred. *Willy Bear.* New York: Parents Maga-
     zine Press, 1976.
     A little boy and his teddy bear prepare for the first day
     in preschool.
105. Katzoff, Betty. *Cathy's First School.* New York: Alfred A.
     Knopf, 1964.
     Realistic portrayal of Cathy's experiences that are
     capped by a birthday party.
106. Mannheim, Grete. *The Two Friends.* New York: Alfred Knopf,
     1968.
     A little girl's shyness, fright, and loneliness on entering
     kindergarten are alleviated when she finds a friend.
107. Rockwell, Harlow. *My Nursery School.* New York: Wm.
     Morrow, 1976.
     Shows a preschool through the eyes of a child at-
     tending it.
108. Steiner, Charlotte. *I'd Rather Stay with You.* New York:
     Seabury Press, 1965.
     A little kangaroo does not want to leave his mother's
     pouch. With the help of his supportive mother, he finally
     goes to kindergarten.

109. Thayer, Jane. *A Drink for Little Red Diker*. New York: William Morrow, 1963.

     A little red deer is ready for some independence but has to overcome his mother's hesitance.

110. Wells, Rosemary. *Timothy Goes to School*. New York: Dial, 1981.

     His first three days in school Timothy tries to make friends with the class perfectionist. But then he makes friends with Violet and begins to enjoy school.

111. Wolde, Gunilla. *Betsy's First Day at Nursery School*. New York: Random House, 1976.

     Shows Betsy's beginning doubts, which are allayed when she makes a friend.

112. Yashima, Tara. *Crow Boy*. New York: Viking, 1955.

     This book has become a classic. It depicts Chibi, a shy boy in rural Japan, who develops a special sensitivity to the sights and sounds around him. A sensitive teacher helps the other children to appreciate Chibi's special talents.

Various Separations

113. Adams, Florence. *Mushy Eggs*. New York: G. P. Putnam, 1973.

     A beloved babysitter leaves for a job overseas.

114. Brown, Myra B. *First Night Away from Home*. New York: Franklin Watts, 1960.

     Stevie is proud of his independence when he goes to sleep in his friend's house. In the evening he is much relieved, however, when his mother brings his favorite toy.

115. Brown, Margaret Wise. *The Runaway Bunny*. Rev. ed. New York: Harper & Row, 1972.

     In this perennial favorite, a little bunny prepares to run away and his mother tells him that she will be there, wherever he goes, for he is her little bunny.

116. Chalmers, Mary. *Be Good Harry*. New York: Harper & Row, 1967.

     A very small cat reluctantly stays with a trusted babysitter, who helps him to overcome his unhappiness. Best of all, his mother returns soon, as she had promised.

117. Cohen, Miriam. *The New Teacher*. New York: Macmillan, 1972.

A group of first graders is most reluctant to part from their old teacher and to accept a new one.

118. Corey, Dorothy. *You Go Away*. Chicago: Albert Whitman, 1976.

Presents separation experiences from early peek-a-boo games to children's entry into school and their coping with the absence of parents overnight.

119. Goffstein, M. D. *Me and My Captain*. New York: Farrar, Straus & Company, 1974.

Explores positive aspects of separation through the eyes of a miniature doll, who imagines life without another doll.

120. Greenfield, Eloise. *First Pink Light*. New York: Thomas Y. Crowell, 1976.

A young black boy wants to stay awake to wait for his father.

121. Harris, Robie H. *Don't Forget to Come Back*. New York: Alfred A. Knopf, 1978.

Annie has a hard time before she accepts the fact that her parents will return and is able to stay with her baby-sitter for the evening.

122. Kroll, Steven. *Is Milton Missing?* New York: Holiday, 1975.

Richard cannot find his dog and remembers the good times they had. The book ends in a happy surprise.

123. Lisker, Sonia O. *Lost*. New York: Harcourt, Brace, Jovanovich, 1975.

Being lost is a frightening separation. When a boy gets lost the world suddenly looks threatening. In the end he not only finds his family but also other helpful adults.

124. Minerik, Else H. *Little Bear's Friends*. New York: Harper & Row, 1960.

Emily has to part from her friend after summer vacation is over.

125. Myers, Bernice. *My Mother Is Lost*. New York: Harcourt Brace & World, 1975.

Depicts the feelings of Jean at being lost.

126. Ormsby, Virginia H. *What's Wrong with Julio?* Philadelphia, Pa.: J. B. Lippincott, 1965.

The children in school are puzzled at Julio's distant behavior until they find out that he misses his parents. Then they decide to help him.

127. Raskin, Ellen. *Moose, Goose, and Little Nobody.* New York: Parents Magazine Press, 1974.

A little mouse, separated from his mother, is no longer sure about who he is.

128. Ross, G. Max. *When Lucy Went Away.* New York: Dutton, 1976.

This sympathetic book depicts children's feelings when their cat disappears on moving day and is not found.

129. Schick, Eleanor. *Katie Goes to Camp.* New York: Macmillan, 1968.

Katie is helped to overcome her uneasiness in camp by attributing her feelings to her doll.

130. Sharmat, Marjorie Weinman. *I Want Mama.* New York: Harper & Row, 1974.

Depicts the sadness of a little girl, whose mother is hospitalized and the warmth of the family when she returns.

131. Simon, Norma. *Benji's Bird.* Chicago: Albert Whitman, 1965.

When Benji nurses an injured robin back to health, he becomes deeply attached to him. Eventually the robin leaves and Benji learns to accept this separation.

132. Sonneborn, Ruth. *I Love Gram.* New York: Viking, 1971.

Depicts the feelings of a little girl, whose grandmother is hospitalized, with realism and sensitivity. Includes a description of the hospital.

133. Stecher, Miriam B. *Daddy and Ben Together.* New York: Lothrop, Lee & Shepard, 1981.

Daddy and Ben take care of each other while mother is away for a few days on business.

134. Steig, William. *Amos and Boris.* New York: Farrar, Straus & Giroux, 1971.

Amos, a mouse, and Boris, a whale, are very close friends. When they were forced to part, their relationship left a lasting effect.

135. Tompert, Ann. *Little Fox Goes to the End of the World*. New York: Crown, 1976.

Depicts the daydreams of Little Fox who can cope with all adventures she meets.

136. Waber, B. *Ira Sleeps Over*. Boston: Houghton Mifflin, 1972.

Ira's first night away from home is made easier by the presence of his Teddy Bear.

137. Whitmore, Martha. *My Friend William Moved Away*. Nashville, Tenn.: Abingdon Press, 1979.

Jimmy is sad when his friend moves away, but then he finds a new friend.

138. Zolotov, Charlotte. *If You Listen*. New York: Harper & Row, 1980.

"A little girl misses her father. He has been gone a long time." This warm book suggests ways of remembering and recalling love.

139. ———. *May I Visit?* New York: Harper & Row, 1976.

Depicts the feelings of a child when the older sibling leaves home.

140. ———. *The Summer Night*. New York: Harper & Row, 1974.

A little girl is cared for by her father while mother is away. They explore the summer evening together.

HOSPITALIZATION AND ILLNESS

Children's reactions to being sick are described by Anna Freud (190) who differentiates between the effects of physical distress and the anxiety it causes on one hand and the effects of nursing care and other adult handling on the other. She notes that even minor illness, not requiring hospitalization, may sometimes result in long-lasting emotional consequences. The emotional climate of the home changes, says Freud, when a young child is sick. Children are confused by the suddenly altered way their parents treat them. Some mothers become more ascetic, letting the child "sleep it out"; others more fussy and indulgent, suspending disciplinary rules. The child's body may be subjected by some well-meaning adults to forced feeding or forced evacuation of his bowels. They are washed and dressed, the way they used to be when they were babies. All this for a child, who has been praised for and proud of his accomplishments, means a loss of independence and a loss of control of his own body. (Incidentally, even adults are often annoyed and humiliated by the infantilizing effect of hospital procedures.) For children, giving up accomplishments means a return to a state they have left only recently. Some children react by becoming "difficult patients." Others will have to be trained anew after they recover, to renounce their new-old babyish ways.

Most children find restriction of movement even harder to take, says Freud, than pain itself. Toddlers have been known to stand up in their cribs until they literally collapse. Older children immobilized after surgery, for instance, often develop tic-like movements and show their irritability through heightened aggression, moodiness, and bad language.

Food restrictions, on the other hand, seem to upset the adult more than the child. Freud suggests that urging or forcing children to eat can have a more negative effect than a temporary loss of appetite. Freud describes the onset of illness occurring in one of two ways: (1) Some children withdraw from the environment. They lie down or curl up in a corner seemingly listless. They concentrate, she says, on their body and its needs by temporarily withdrawing from the world. (2) Other children become clinging and babyish, demanding a surplus of love, attention, and coddling.

The blows to the as yet shaky self-image of children can be as traumatic as the illness itself. In fact, some children are considered "changed" after some mild tonsillitis or other common illness. These changes can be manifested in mood swings, changes in relationships to parents or siblings, temper tantrums, regression to bedwetting or soiling, feeding or sleeping problems, school phobias or changes in school performance.

Psychological stress is increased further if the child is hospitalized. Haller, Talbert, and Dombro (162) suggest that in cases of minor surgery, for instance, the damages of psychological traumas are far greater than the dangers of physiological complications. John Bowlby (152, 153) describes eloquently the acute distress that children can feel even if only hospitalized for a short while. There are several factors that contribute to the shattering effect hospitalization can have. Separation from trusted adults, a strange, frightening environment, impersonal, uncomfortable, or painful procedures all contribute (182, 183, 204, 205, 206, 213). In addition, children are acutely conscious of the fright, anxiety, and helplessness of their parents. Sigal (208) found, for instance, that children whose parents thought they might die had much more frequent behavior disturbances.

In recent years medical and nursing literature has focused with far-reaching effect on the emotional care of the hospitalized child (141, 143, 144, 145, 146, 147, 148, 149, 151, 154, 158, 162, 163, 172, 173, 175, 176, 177, 179, 180, 181, 182, 184, 185, 186, 188, 193, 194, 195, 196, 197, 198, 203, 205, 206, 207, 209, 211). This awareness brought about many changes. Parents are increasingly encouraged to be present and to participate in some form in the child's care (181, 185, 191, 192, 193, 195). In fact, after strenuously resisting the invasion of their territory, at first, nurses find that parents on the ward can be useful adjuncts (193). "Humanizing" the handling of children in hospitals is discussed by many authors (150, 151, 158, 162, 166, 175). Such humanizing includes play programs for hospitalized children and clinic patients (147, 154, 156, 172). Play for children is not just entertainment. It provides the means for emotional and intellectual "digesting" of new and painful experiences. Children allowed to look at what's happening to them from the outside, as it were, are not only better able to cope, they can gain additional strength in the process.

A number of hospitals now have programs aimed at making equipment and procedures more familiar (199, 201, 211, 212). Familiarity can be facilitated by books depicting hospital experiences and equipment and by explaining strange procedures and unfamiliar terminology (215, 219, 220, 221, 222, 224, 226, 228, 229, 230, 231, 232, 233, 235, 237, 240, 242, 244, 245, 251, 252). Such books can be helpful before, during, and after illness. In addition to being illuminating about hospital facts, books can be helpful in opening up communication about feelings. Bibliotherapy—a comparatively new field—focuses especially on the emotional relief books can provide (141, 157, 160, 177). Books describing emotions about illness and hospitalization are well represented in the section dealing with children's books (216, 217, 218, 223, 225, 226, 227, 229, 230, 236, 239, 241, 243, 244, 245, 246, 248, 249, 250, 251); they include not only the feelings and reactions of the patient but describe feelings of family members and friends as well.

Schools can play a major role in preparing children for hospitalization and in helping them to work through their experiences and feelings after illness (149, 164, 167, 169, 183, 187, 210). Here again, play as well as listening to stories are the means that help children to come to grips with stressful facts. Most pre-schools encourage dramatic play. Providing for doctor play and hospital play by providing stimulating props, such as stethoscopes, needle-less syringes, etc., will allow children to think about their experiences and fantasies.

Long-term illness or hospitalization are discussed by Spinetta et al. (176) and by Pearse (202). Both authors emphasize the child's need for a life as close to normal as possible, in spite of the illness.

The needs and problems of the sick child's parents are beginning to be recognized (143, 144, 196, 198, 207, 208). In fact, literature acknowledges that brothers, sisters, and other family members have a difficult time as well (188, 196, 209). It is at this time of fear, panic, and crisis that parents have to provide major support to their ill child. It is, therefore, essential that they, in turn, receive support and understanding from the helping professions.

BIBLIOGRAPHY

Books and Pamphlets for Adults

141. Altshuler, Anne. *Books That Help Children with a Hospital Experience.* HSA 74-5402. Rockville, Md.: Public Health Service, Health Service Administration, U.S. Department of Health, Education, and Welfare, 1974. ERIC Documents Reproduction Service ED 115 375.

Provides an excellent bibliography that lists books according to the age for which they are appropriate, rates them for quality, and gives short synopses of plots.

142. Anthony, James E., and Koupernik, Cyrille. *The Child in His Family: The Impact of Disease and Death.* Yearbook of the International Association for Child Psychiatry and Allied Professions. Vol. 2. New York: John Wiley & Sons, 1973.

Contains articles by outstanding authorities on problems in connection with illness.

143. Association for the Care of Children's Health (AACH). *A Child Goes to the Hospital.* Washington, D.C.: Author, 1981.

This pamphlet helps parents to be better prepared for their child's hospitalization by recognizing their own feelings and giving their child the understanding and support it needs.

144. ———. *Preparing Your Child for Repeated or Extended Hospitalizations.* Washington, D.C.: Author, 1982.

Discusses the feelings parents and children face. Gives valuable suggestions for parents to help themselves as well as their child.

145. ———. *The Chronically Ill Child and Family in the Community.* Washington, D.C.: Author, 1982.

Discusses many important topics such as family relations, managing medical care, dealing with the community, and schools and finances.

146. ———. *Activities for Children with Special Needs.* Washington, D.C.: Author, 1980.

Describes many activities for children with motor, sight, hearing, and respiratory difficulties.

147. ———. *Ideas for Activities with Hospitalized Children.* Washington, D.C.: Author, 1970.

Contains many suggestions of games, crafts, "reenactment" play, and outpatient projects.

148. ———. *Preparing Children and Families for Health Care Encounters.* Washington, D.C.: Author, 1980.

This pamphlet presents a compilation of pertinent articles for parents and professionals.

149. ———. *A Guide for Teachers: Children and Hospitals.* Washington, D.C.: Author, 1981.

This pamphlet gives suggestions to preschool and elementary teachers on preparing children for hospital care.

150. Bergman, Thesi, and Freud, Anna. *Children in the Hospital.* New York: International Universities Press, 1966.

Urges an organized technique of "mental first aid" in the hospital which involves not only patients and their parents but nursing and medical staff as well.

151. Beuf, Ann Hill. *Biting Off the Bracelet: A Study of Children in Hospitals.* Philadelphia, Pa.: University of Pennsylvania Press, 1979.

Reviews poor conditions of children still prevalent in many hospitals where efficient operation seems more important than helping children and psychological know-how is used only to adjust the child to the existing environment. Theoretical discussion and field observations.

152. Bowlby, John. *Attachment and Loss.* Vol. 1: *Attachment.* New York: Basic Books, 1969.

153. ———. *Attachment and Loss*. Vol. 2: *Separation*. New York: Basic Books, 1973.

These books contain important references contributed by a man who pioneered studies of separation and young children. The material about young children in hospitals is particularly eloquent, as are the films Bowlby and James Robertson made on this subject.

154. Child Life Department, I. W. K. Hospital for Children. *Play with Me*. Halifax, N.S., Canada, n.d.

Pamphlet includes games and stimuli for infants at home or in the hospital.

155. Comer, James P., and Poussaint, Alvin F. *Black Child Care: How to Bring up a Healthy Black Child*. New York: Pocket Books, 1975.

Written in question-and-answer form, it gives understanding advice on helping children with illness and hospitalization.

156. The Early Childhood Care Department of Vanier College. *Ideas for Your Child*. Laurent, Quebec, Canada, n.d.

Pamphlet describes play activities and inexpensive materials that provide enjoyable and stimulating experience with a child in hospital.

157. Fassler, Joan. *Helping Children Cope: Mastering Stress Through Books and Stories*. New York: Free Press, 1978.

Presents the use of children's literature as a help in coping with stressful experiences. The chapter on hospitalization and illness contains a sensitive discussion and review of children's books and general references.

158. Geist, Harold. *A Child Goes to Hospital: The Psychological Aspects of a Child Going to Hospital*. Springfield, Ill.: Charles C Thomas, 1965.

Urges "humanization" of the hospital, offering guidelines to prevent or reduce emotional damage to children.

159. Government Printing Office. *A Reader's Guide: For Parents of Children with Mental, Physical, or Emotional Disabilities*. Publication No. (HSA) 77-5290.

An undated reference on basic readings and books that deal with playing at home and other issues. Includes books written by parents and children.

160. ———. *Books That Help Children Deal with a Hospital Experience*. Publication No. (HSA) 78-5524.

Annotated listing of books that deal with children and hospitals.

161. ———. *When Your Child Goes to the Hospital*. Publication No. (OHDS) 793-30092. Available free.

Gives detailed guide to parents and family members, including definitions of terms and references.

162. Haller, Jacob Alexander, ed.; Talbert, James L.; and Dumbro, Robert H., asst. eds. *The Hospitalized Child and His Family*. Baltimore, Md.: Johns Hopkins University Press, 1967.

Written for professionals in the field of medicine but of interest to all because of its humane approach. This book covers preparation for surgery, play in the hospital, the return home, and much more.

163. Hardgrove, Carol, and Dawson, Rosemary. *Parents and Children in the Hospital*. Boston, Mass.: Little Brown, 1972.

Describes the unique contributions families can make in ensuring the emotional well-being of children in hospital settings.

164. Hendrick, Joanne. *The Whole Child: New Trends in Early Education*. 2d ed. St. Louis, Mo.: The C. V. Mosby Company, 1980.

Discusses preparation for hospitalization in school, dealing with classmates and helping the child and his parents during hospitalization. Also handles the problems that arise when a parent is hospitalized.

165. Kellerman, Jonathan. *Helping the Fearful Child: A Guide to Everyday and Problem Anxieties*. New York: W. W. Norton, 1981.

Provides helpful answers to parents faced with children's fears and anxieties. Provides clear distinction between "normal" fears and those that indicate a need for professional help.

166. Kliman, Gilbert. *Psychological Emergencies of Childhood*. New York: Grune & Stratton, 1968.

Discusses the emotional factors of illness, preparation for hospitalization and psychological help for dying children.

167. McCarthy, Jan. "Coping with a New Environment." In *Helping Children Cope with Change*, edited by Sandra M. Long and Barbara Batchelor, pp. 21–25. Terre Haute, Ind.: Indiana Association for the Education of Young Children, 1979.

Discusses ways children can be helped to accept new environments, including hospitals.

168. McCollum, Audrey T. *Coping with Prolonged Health Impairments in Your Child*. Boston, Mass.: Little, Brown & Company, 1975.

An understanding and supportive book for families of a child with acute or chronic illness. Discusses feelings and attitudes and gives sound, practical advice.

169. Murphy, Lois B., and Leeper, Ethel M. *Preparing for Change*. DHEW Publication CD 73-1028. Washington, D.C.: U.S. Department of Health, Education, and Welfare, 1973.

Discusses the preschool's role in helping children who have to go to hospital or to get "shots."

170. Oremland, Evelyn K., and Oremland, Jerome D. *The Effects of Hospitalization on Children*. Springfield, Ill.: Charles C Thomas, 1973.

Suggests various means of facilitating emotional as well as physical recovery and rehabilitation.

171. Petrillo, Madeline, and Sanger, Sirgay. *Emotional Care of Hospitalized Children: An Environmental Approach*. Philadelphia, Pa.: J. B. Lippincott, 1980.

Describes what can be done to meet the emotional needs of children. Gives specific suggestions.

172. Plank, Emma N. *Working with Children in Hospitals*. Rev. 2d ed. Cleveland: The Press of Case Western Reserve University, 1971.

Offers a sensitive discussion of how children feel when hospitalized and how staff and parents can help them adjust to the experience. Advocates play activities and equipment to help children deal with the hospitalization experience.

173. Pomerantz, Virginia E., and Schultz, Dodi. *The First Five Years: A Relaxed Approach to Child Care.* Garden City, N.Y.: Doubleday, 1973.

     Wise counsel from a pediatrician about everyday problems, including sickness and hospitalization.

174. Robinson, Geoffrey C., and Clark, Heather F. *The Hospital Care of Children: A Review of Contemporary Issues.* New York: Oxford University Press, 1980.

     Presents a comprehensive review of the literature pertaining to child- and family-oriented hospital care. Discusses alternative care, such as home care, parent care, day hospitals, ambulatory surgery, and outpatient assessment. Reviews programs that provide play, preparation, and educational hospital experiences.

175. Shore, Milton F., ed. *Red Is the Color of Hurting: Planning for Children in the Hospital.* Bethesda, Md.: National Institute of Mental Health (NIMH), 1965.

     Urges reduction of emotional stress for the hospitalized child.

176. Spinetta, John J., Deasy, Patricia M., Koenig, Harold M., Lightsey, Alton L., Schwarz, Donald B., Hartman, Gary A., and Kung, Faith H. *Talking with Children with a Life-Threatening Illness: A Handbook for Health Care Professionals.* ERIC Document Reproduction Service, ED 178 213, 1979.

     The objective of this booklet is to enable the child to live as normal a life as possible in spite of the illness.

177. U.S. Department of Health, Education, and Welfare. Public Health Service/Health Services Administration. *Books That Help Children Deal with a Hospital Experience.* Rev. ed. Publication 017-031-00020-1. Rockville, Md.: USDHEW, 1978.

     Listing of books for children that discuss hospitalization and illness. Gives full publishing information, recommended age levels, description of contents, and rates books from excellent to poor.

178. Wolff, Sula. *Children under Stress.* Rev. ed. Baltimore, Md.: Penguin Books, 1973.

     Chapter on illness and going to hospital discusses psychological implications of illness, the impact of the hospital experience and other major stresses. Provides guidelines for reducing stress by talking about fears and worries.

Studies and Articles

179. Aiken, Marcia A. "Flight, Fight, or . . . ." *Journal of the Association for the Care of Children in Hospitals,* Summer 1978, pp. 23–27.

    Describes changes effected in a pediatric unit through the effort of two mothers.

180. Audette, M. S. "The Significance of Regressive Behavior for the Hospitalized Child." *Maternal Child Nursing Journal* 3 (1974):31–40.

    Discussion of regression in children as a reaction to the stress of hospitalization.

181. Bowden, Marita S. "How We Did It: Family Centered Care in a Large Community Hospital." *Journal of the Association for the Care of Children in Hospitals,* Summer 1979, pp. 14–17.

    Description of a family-centered program in a large hospital that includes pediatrics and maternity.

182. Branstetter, Ellamae. "The Young Child's Response to Hospitalization: Separation Anxiety or Lack of Mothering Care." *American Journal of Public Health* 59 (1969): 92–96.

    Suggests that some toddler reactions are due to lack of mothering care rather than the absence of the parent.

183. Butler, Annie L. "Tender Topics: Children and Crisis." ERIC Document Reproduction Service, ED 147 019, 1977.

    Discusses children's responses to stressful events and describes feelings about and reactions to hospitalization and other separations as related to age differences. These are discussed in terms of general cognitive development and developmental stages. Suggests that adults can help children cope with crisis situations by providing accurate information, by encouraging the expression of feelings and by managing their own feelings and attitudes toward these same events. Ways in which outside supportive services, teachers, initial family relationships, and family life education can affect the child's responses to a crisis situation are also described.

184. Calkin, Joy D. "Are Hospitalized Toddlers Adapting to the Experience as Well as We Think?" *American Journal of Maternal Child Nursing*, January/February 1979, pp. 18–23.

Provides means to assess the emotional adaptation of toddlers.

185. Dumbro, Robert H. "The Surgically Ill Child and His Family." *Surgical Clinics of North America* 50 (1970):759–768.

Description of a family-centered program that aims to support the family and the patient.

186. Droske, Susan C. "Children's Behavioral Changes Following Hospitalization—Have We Prepared the Parents?" *Journal of the Association for the Care of Children in Hospitals*, Fall 1978, pp. 3–7.

Description of post-hospitalization behavior changes due to anxiety.

187. Engdahl, Jane. "Dealing with a Child's Previous Hospitalization on Re-entry to School." In *When There Is a Crisis*, edited by Sandra M. Long and Barbara Batchelor, eds., pp. 42–47. Terre Haute, Inc.: Indiana Association for the Education of Young Children, 1979.

Helps teachers to prepare their class for the child's re-entry and to minimize the ex-patient's difficulties.

188. Everson, Sally. "Sibling Counseling." *American Journal of Nursing*, 1977, pp. 644–646.

Describes the impact of chronic illness of a child on siblings.

189. Fassler, David. "The Young Child in Hospital." *Young Children* 35 (1980):19–25.

Helps parents and teachers to clear up misconceptions children often have about hospitalization.

190. Freud, Anna. "The Role of Bodily Illness in the Mental Life of Children." In *Psychoanalytic Study of the Child*, pp. 69–81. Vol. 7. New York: International Universities Press, 1952.

Classic outline of the effects of bodily illness. Differentiates between the effects of nursing care and medical procedures on one hand and those of pain and anxiety on the other.

191. Goldson, Edward. "The Family Care Center: Transitional Care for the Sick Infant and His Family." *Children Today* 10 (July/August 1981):15.

Describes a hospital program where sick newborns, not any more in need of intensive care, having reached physical stability, are moved to a "Family Care Center" where parents can spend as much time as they wish. The center neither increased risk of infection nor did it prolong hospitalization or prove costly. A follow-up clinic with an interdisciplinary team completes the program.

192. Green, Morris, and Green, Janice G. "The Parent Care Pavillion." *Children Today* 7 (September/October 1977):5.

Describes a facility for toddlers within a hospital where parents are encouraged to play a major role.

193. Hardgrove, Carol, and Rutledge, Ann. "Parenting During Hospitalization." *American Journal of Nursing* 75 (1975): 836–838.

Description of a pediatric program, where parents are considered useful adjuncts to the nursing staff.

194. Hennessey, J. A. "Hospitalized Toddlers' Responses to Mothers' Tape Recordings During Brief Separations." *Maternal Child Nursing Journal* 5 (1976):69–91.

Description of a study where the recorded voice of the mother was used to soothe toddlers.

195. Hill, Carol Schnaidt. "The Mother on the Pediatric Ward: Insider or Outlawed?" *Pediatric Nursing*, September/October 1978, pp. 26–29.

Discusses how to implement parent participation in the hospital care of children.

196. Isner, N. "The Family of the Hospitalized Child." *Nursing Clinics of North America* 7 (1972):5–12.

Discusses the impact of the hospitalization of a child on the total family unit: the patient, the parents, and the siblings.

197. James, F. E. "Behavior Reactions of Normal Children to Common Illnesses Treated at Home." *The Practitioner* 188 (1962):670–674.

Found that children often develop behavior disorders after a stressful illness.

198. Jay, Susan Schaeffer. "Pediatric Intensive Care: Involving

Parents in the Care of Their Child." *Maternal Child Nursing Journal* 6 (1977):195–203.

Description of parents' reaction to the pediatric intensive care unit with helpful suggestions.

199. Johnson, Beverley H. "Before Hospitalization: A Preparation Program for the Child and His Family." *Children Today* 3 (1974):18–21.

Describes the development of a preparation program prior to hospitalization.

200. Johnson, Melissa Ramirez; Barclay, Martin; Whitt, J. Kenneth; and Weisz, John. "Anxiety Reduction Through Fantasy in Chronically Ill Children." ERIC Document Reproduction Service, ED 195 868, 1980.

Chronically ill children were significantly more anxious than the healthy children. Fantasy facilitation was found to be effective in reducing anxiety for both groups.

201. Klein, Doris. "Rx for Pediatric Patients: Play While You Wait." *Young Children* 34 (1979):13–19.

Describes a children's activity program at a pediatric clinic in the University of Colorado Medical Center. The program focuses on helping to ease children's anxieties and counteract their misconceptions about medical visits through play.

202. Pearse, Martha. "The Child with Cancer; Impact on the Family." *Journal of School Health* 43, no. 3 (1977):174–179.

Finds that the family of a child with cancer is faced with special adjustment problems that must be confronted, including guilt, anger, and a desire to retain a sense of normalcy.

203. Roskies, Ethel; Bedard, Paul; Grauvreau-Gilbault, Helene; and Lafortune, Danielle. "Emergency Hospitalization of Young Children: Some Neglected Psychological Considerations." *Medical Care* 13 (1975):570–581.

Found that children with emergency admission were subjected to more physical and psychological trauma than elective admissions.

204. Rosoff, Barbara. "'Mommy Went Away Because I Was Bad': When a Parent Is Institutionalized." In *Helping Children Cope with Change*, edited by Sandra M. Long and Barbara Batchelor, pp. 33–41. Terre Haute, Ind.: Indiana Association for the Education of Young Children, 1979.

Gives helpful explanations and suggestions to caregivers of children whose parents are hospitalized, imprisoned, or separated due to other reasons.

205. Rutter, Michael. "Separation Experiences: A New Look at an Old Topic." *The Journal of Pediatrics* 95 (1980):147–154.

Pleads for a more differentiated look at separations, considering children's age, temperament, and previous experiences. Some separations can indicate psychiatric risks.

206. Schmeltz, K. "An Early Latency Child's Use of Obsessional Ritual to Master Separation Anxiety." *Maternal Child Nursing Journal* 6 (1977):117–134.

Case study of preschool separation anxiety and rituals as means to relieve separation anxiety.

207. Seegel, Virginia F. "The Divorced Parent and the Hospitalized Child: Implications for the Hospital Staff." *Journal of the Association for the Care of Children in Hospitals*, Fall 1978, pp. 16–18.

Describes the additional stresses on the single parent of a hospitalized child.

208. Sigal, John J. "Enduring Disturbances in Behavior Following Acute Illness in Early Childhood: Consistencies in Four Independent Follow-up Studies." In *The Child in His Family: Children at Psychiatric Risk*, edited by E. James Anthony and Cyrille Koupernik, pp. 415–424. Yearbook of the International Association for Child Psychiatry and Allied Professions. Vol. 3. New York: John Wiley & Sons, 1944.

Found frequent behavior problems among children whose parents had felt the child might die.

209. Spivack, Mayer. "Helping a Child in the Hospital: A Father's Story." *Journal of the Association for the Care of Children in Hospitals*, Winter 1979, pp. 11–13.

Describes the way the fears of an older brother were relieved by means of the recorded voice of the hospitalized child.

210. Stein, Myron; Beyer, Evelyn; and Ronald, Doris. "Beyond Benevolence: The Mental Health Role of the Preschool Teacher." *Young Children* 30 (1975):358–372.

Argues for an increased mental health role of preschool teachers at a time when parents might be overwhelmed by their problems.

211. Visintainer, Madelon A., and Wolfer, John A. "Psychological Preparations for Surgical Pediatric Patients: The Effect on Children's and Parents' Stress Responses and Adjustment." *Pediatrics* 56 (1975):187–202.

Found that preparation and support increase children's cooperation and decrease their upset behavior and at the same time reduce anxiety in parents.

212. West, Anne R. "Bringing the Hospital to Preschoolers: Teaching Young Children About Hospitals and Health Care." *Children Today* 7 (March–April 1978):16.

Describes a program sponsored by Children's Hospital, National Medical Center in Washington, D.C. that teaches young children about hospitals. Volunteers visit preschools, read a story, show pictures, demonstrate equipment, and encourage children to use the equipment in dramatic play.

213. Yarrow, Leon J. "Separation from Parents During Early Childhood." In *Review of Child Development Research*, edited by Martin L. Hoffman and Lois Wladis Hoffman, Vol. 1., pp. 89–136. New York: Russell Sage Foundation, 1964.

Summary of research, analyzing factors that affect children's reactions to various separations from parents, i.e., day care, institutionalization, multiple mothering, hospitalization, maternal employment and father separation.

214. Zambana, Ruth E.; Hurst, Marsha; and Hite, Rodney L. "The Working Mother in Contemporary Perspective: A Review of the Literature." *Pediatrics* 64 (1979):862–868.

Provides an overview of research which should help teachers and other professionals who counsel working mothers and their families.

Books for Children

215. Althea. *Going into Hospital*. Cambridge, England: Dinosaur Publications, 1974.

Brief, simple book that introduces a number of children hospitalized for various reasons. While pain and discomfort are not denied, each child seems to be able to manage his discomfort.

216. Association for the Care of Children's Health. *Becky's Story.* Washington, D.C.: Author, 1981.

Addresses the siblings of the hospitalized child. Helps brothers and sisters to understand their own needs and feelings through Becky's experiences.

217. Bemelmans, Ludwig. *Madeline.* New York: Viking, 1967.

The story of Madeline's appendectomy has become a modern classic.

218. Brandenburg, Franz. *I Wish I Was Sick, Too!* New York: Macmillan, 1978.

Animal characters tell the story of a sister who wishes for the extra attention her sick brother received—until she also becomes sick. They learn about nurturing others and agree that getting well is the best part of being sick.

219. Breinburg, Petronella. *Doctor Shawn.* New York: Thomas Y. Crowell, 1975.

Equipped with toy props and vivid imaginations, children play hospital, bandaging limbs and dispensing banana-slice pills.

220. Children's Hospital of Philadelphia. *Danny's Heart Operation.* Philadelphia, Pa.: Children's Hospital, 1976.

A matter-of-fact, detailed account of Danny's experiences in hospital and after.

221. ———. *Dee Dee's Heart Test.* Philadelphia, Pa.: Children's Hospital, 1976.

Step-by-step experiences of a little girl undergoing cardiac catherization.

222. Elder, Barbara Schuyler Haas. *The Hospital Book.* 4th ed. Baltimore, Md.: The John Street Press, 1975.

Coloring book that presents pleasant and unpleasant experiences in hospital. Includes admission procedures, most common procedures and diagrams of major organs and bones.

223. Fassler, Joan. *The Boy with a Problem.* New York: Behavioral Publications, 1971.

Concentrates on Johnny's feelings and reactions, never

specifying his "problem." Johnny gets better when he gets the serious attention of his friend.

224. Howe, James. *The Hospital Book.* New York: Crown, 1981.

Factual presentation of commonly used hospital equipment and procedures with the explanations and photographs. The major message is that hospital staff cares about children.

225. Lexau, Joan M. *Benjie on His Own.* New York: Dial, 1970.

Describes Benjie's feelings when his grandmother is taken to hospital by ambulance.

226. Marino, Barbara Pavis. *Eric Needs Stitches.* Reading, Mass.: Addison Wesley, 1979.

A bicycle accident necessitates Eric's first trip to the hospital. Adults are supportive throughout Eric's honest reactions—nausea, a desire to run away, trembling, yelling, etc.

227. McPhail, David. *The Bear's Toothache.* Boston: Little Brown, 1972.

Shows Little Bear's reactions when his tooth hurts.

228. Odor, Ruth. *Brian's Trip to the Hospital.* Cincinnati, Ohio: Standard Publishing, 1977.

Describes Brian's tonsillectomy beginning with going to the hospital and including post-operative discomfort. Christian orientation.

229. Rey, Margaret, and Rey, H. A. *Curious George Goes to Hospital.* Boston: Houghton Mifflin, 1966.

Curious George's stay in hospital serves as a nonthreatening introduction to the world of hospitals.

230. Rockwell, Anne, and Rockwell, Harlow. *Sick in Bed.* New York: Macmillan, 1982.

Written in first person, a little boy gives a graphic description of a short tonsillitis with high fever and how he felt about it.

231. Rockwell, Harlow. *My Doctor.* New York: Macmillan, 1973.

232. ———. *My Dentist.* New York: Greenwillow Books, 1975.

Both books describe visits to woman doctors. Emphasis is on clear descriptions of procedures.

233. Scarry, Richard. *Richard Scarry's Nicky Goes to the Doctor.* Racine, Wisc.: Western Publishing, 1971.

    Nicky Bunny has a complete check-up.

234. Segal, Lore. *Tell Me a Mitzi.* New York: Farrar, Straus & Giroux, 1970.

    Contains three family stories. In one of them a whole family has the sniffles.

235. Shay, Arthur. *What Happens When You Go to the Hospital.* Chicago, Ill.: Reilly & Lee, 1969.

    Karen, a black seven-year-old has a tonsillectomy.

236. Sharmat, Marjorie Weinman. *I Want Mama.* New York: Harper & Row, 1974.

    Depicts the sadness of a little girl whose mother is hospitalized and the warmth of the family when she returns.

237. Showers, Paul. *No Measles, No Mumps for Me.* New York: Thomas Y. Crowell, 1980.

    Provides an elementary explanation of immunizations: what happens when bacteria and viruses invade, the role of white cells and antibodies, and how booster drops and shots are administered.

238. Silverstein, Alvin, and Silverstein, Virginia B. *Itch, Sniffle, and Sneeze: All About Asthma, Hay Fever, and Other Allergies.* New York: Four Winds Press, 1978.

    Offers a factual discussion on allergies and their causes that should be illuminating to young children.

239. Smith, Grace, compiler. *The Hospital Is Where . . . .* Manhattan Beach, Calif., 1975.

    Compilation of writings and drawings of children, who experienced hospitalization. Pathetic and funny, this book can be helpful to children who also have to cope.

240. Sobol, Harriet Langsam. *Jeff's Hospital Book.* New York: Walck, 1975.

    Photographic documentation of Jeff's two-night hospital stay from admission to discharge.

241. Sonneborn, Ruth. *I Love Gram.* New York: Viking, 1971.

    Depicts the feelings of a little girl whose grandmother is hospitalized, with realism and sensitivity. Includes a description of the hospital.

242. Steedman, Julie. *Emergency Room: An ABC Tour.* McLean, Va.: EPM Publications, 1974.

Photographs of emergency room scenes accompanied by brief definitions and explanations. Children of all ages in various stages of treatment are introduced during this ABC tour of the emergency room.

243. Stein, Sara Bonnett. *About Handicaps.* New York: Walker & Company, 1974.

Matthew reacts with fear to Joe's "crooked" legs. Matthew's father helps him to build up a positive relationship.

244. ———. *A Hospital Story.* Open Family Series. New York: Walker & Company, 1974.

Jill anticipates, experiences, and relives being hospitalized for a tonsillectomy. Her fears, anger, and possible misunderstandings are presented through dual adult and child texts and realistic black and white photography.

245. Thomas, Dawn C. *Pablito's New Feet.* Philadelphia, Pa.: J. B. Lippincott, 1973.

A little Puerto Rican boy spends a long time in hospital for corrective surgery after he was crippled by polio. Includes a large warm family and minority group members among hospital staff and patients.

246. Tobias, Tobi. *A Day Off.* New York: G. P. Putnam's Sons, 1973.

A slightly sick boy enjoys staying home and being pampered.

247. Vigna, Judith. *Gregory's Stitches.* Chicago: A. Whitman, 1974.

While saving his parents from man-eating lions, Gregory is injured and needs six stitches, or so the story evolves as retold by his admiring friends.

248. Wahl, Jan. *Doctor Rabbit.* New York: Delacorte Press, 1970.

Doctor Rabbit is a warm, caring doctor, who takes care of his fellow animals. When he gets sick, the animals look after him.

249. Watson, Jane Werner; Switzer, Robert E.; and Hirschberg, J. Cotter. *My Friend the Dentist.* New York: Golden Press, 1972.

250. ———. *My Friend the Doctor.* New York: Golden Press, 1972.

Both books offer some important information and portray some honest feelings.

251. Watts, Marjorie-Ann. *Crocodile Medicine.* New York: Frederick Warne, 1977.

Julie gets cheered up when Crocodile joins her long hospital stay and expresses his feelings about hospital life.

252. Weber, Alfons. *Elisabeth Gets Well.* New York: Thomas Y. Crowell, 1970.

Elisabeth goes to hospital for an appendectomy. Detailed description of procedures. Warm, caring nurses and siblings.

253. Wiseman, Bernard. *Morris Has a Cold.* New York: Dodd Mead, 1978.

Boris the Bear tries to help Morris the Moose to get well.

254. Welzenbach, John F., and Cline, Nancy. *Wendy Well and Billy Better Say "Hello Hospital."* Chicago, Ill.: Med-Educator, 1970.

255. ———. *Wendy Well and Billy Better Visit the Hospital See-Through Machine.* Chicago, Ill.: Med-Educator, 1970.

256. ———. *Wendy Well and Billy Better Meet the Hospital Sandman.* Chicago, Ill.: Med-Educator, 1970.

257. ———. *Wendy Well and Billy Better Ask a "Mill-Yun" Hospital Questions.* Chicago, Ill.: Med-Educator, 1970.

Series of books that give a well-balanced, realistic look at hospitals through the eyes of two children.

258. Wolde, Gunilla. *Betsy and the Chicken Pox.* New York: Random House, 1976.

Betsy feels neglected when her baby brother has the chicken pox.

259. ———. *Betsy and the Doctor.* New York: Random House, 1978.

Betsy needs three stitches after a fall on the playground.

260. ———. *Tommy Goes to the Doctor.* Boston: Houghton Mifflin, 1972.

Tommy and his mother visit a woman doctor. Simple explanations of procedures help Tommy not to feel too afraid.

261. Wolff, Angelika. *Mom! I Broke My Arm!* New York: The Lion Press, 1969.

Steven breaks his arm, has a cast put on in the doctor's office and has it removed after six weeks.

262. Ziegler, Sandra. *At the Hospital: A Surprise for Krissy.* Elgin, Ill.: The Child's World, 1976.

Krissy goes to hospital for a tonsillectomy. Full description of procedures. Krissy enjoys her black roommate. The staff includes a male nurse.

DEATH AND BEREAVEMENT

A preschool teacher came to school one morning and found the pet guinea pig dead in his cage. Quickly, before the children arrived, she wrapped him in newspaper and disposed of the body in the building's incinerator. She was sure that by so doing she would save the children from the horror of death. However, when the children were told of the guinea pig's death their first response was to ask what happened to the body. The teacher told them honestly about the way she disposed of it. The children were furious! "I wanted to see him when he was dead." "I wanted to touch him." Not only did the teacher predict their response erroneously, she also deprived them of a learning experience.

Adults, especially urban, middle-class American adults, often try to shield children from knowledge of death. This desire may be rooted in the same dream of "childhood innocence" that makes it hard to talk about other realities, such as sex, money, friction between parents, and so forth. It may be a reflection of the adult's reluctance to come to terms with the idea of death, his own and that of others. Most certainly adults misjudge children's intellectual development and emotional needs when they think that avoiding the subject is in the interest of the child.

Furman (312) points out that the difference between alive and not-alive becomes clear to young children as they contemplate the difference between a baby and a teddy bear. Even toddlers have been observed to show a keen interest in dead things. They find dead flies and note that they do not move. It is difficult for young children to acquire genuine understanding of death from insects or small animals, however, because they have little emotional significance. The loss of a beloved pet is often the first encounter children have with death (287, 318, 332). Fraiberg (270) describes an incident where a child's hamster died and the parent rushed to replace it in order to minimize the child's shock and grief. Such action, says Fraiberg, conveys to the child, "Don't feel badly; your love is not important; all hamsters, all dogs, all cats are replaceable, and you can love one as well as the others." Children, says Fraiberg, need to experience their grief, to mourn for the dead hamster. The time to buy a new one is when mourning has done its work and the child is ready to attach himself to a new pet.

As this anecdote illustrates, it is not possible to grasp death intellectually and not to involve deep feelings. Nevertheless, according to Furman, children who at the time of bereavement had a grasp of concrete facts, i.e., that death means no life, no eating, no sleeping, no pain, no movement, had a much easier time coping emotionally.

The cognitive development of children as they grasp the concept of death is described by a number of authors (282, 283 290, 300, 307, 312, 320, 327, 328, 330). Sahler (290) points out that preschool children consider death a temporary condition as exemplified by the preschooler who picked up the toy telephone and called "Doctor, come quick, somebody is dead!" Hendrick (276) describes a little boy whose grandfather had died soon after he had found his dog lying dead in the gutter. The child started insisting on walking along the edge of the curb wherever he went, looking—as it turned out—for his dead grandfather! This anecdote, says Hendrick, illustrates Piaget's concept of *assimilation* and *accommodation*. The child *assimilated* his grandfather's death, i.e., he interpreted it in terms of what he knew already from the death of his dog, but was unable to *accommodate* to it, because he lacked the prior knowledge that dead people are not found, usually, in gutters.

McDonald (323) found that children were unable to direct themselves to aspects of their own loss, or to feel sympathy for the loss of a peer until they gained some concrete understanding of what death means.

When dealing with bereaved children, especially with children who have lost a parent, the main danger is that of lasting distortions that can affect development into fully functioning adulthood (290, 303, 305, 312, 323). Furman finds that children who had been exposed to bearable separations, such as a well-handled age-appropriate adjustment to preschool, have built up some strengths toward bearing up under other separations. All authors agree that only if children are helped to recognize their feelings and to express them appropriately, will they be able to cope with them. Bowlby (304, 305) describes children's mourning in three stages: protest, despair, and denial. Bowlby suggests that children will overcome loss only if they form substitute relationships.

Fassler (269) maintains that children respond to the death of an important person with disbelief and denial first; later the child will need considerable time discussing and remembering the person who died. Among the feelings the child experiences will be ambivalent feelings including anger for having been abandoned. There may also be feelings of guilt, since children often believe that a momentary thought, dream, or wish has caused a beloved person to die. Eventually, as mourning does its work and the child recovers, he will become able to form substitute relationships.

Bereaved children's ability to deal with their loss will also depend on the emotional reactions of the adults around them, particularly of the surviving parent (299). Since that parent is, understandably, under great stress, helpful support by a trusted teacher (276, 306, 307, 312, 314, 333) or other supportive adult (279, 296, 307, 326, 327) can be of enormous significance and help.

It would be desirable if children could talk about death, express their feelings, and have their questions answered without having to cope with the stress of loss (272, 287). Some adults will find methods based on *bibliotherapy*, i.e., discussions following the reading of a story written for children. These methods are described by various authors (264, 265, 269, 289, 310) who all include suggested books. A number of appropriate children's books (336–361) are included in this section.

Death does not always occur suddenly. Children may have to be told that their parent is fatally ill. Such honest explanations can diminish the child's feelings of guilt and reestablish an emotional closeness with the dying person that will make both of them feel better.

It is even harder for a parent to face the terminal illness of a child than it is for a child to lose a parent. Futterman and Hoffman (313) state that the dying child produces a prolonged crisis for his parents. Lascari and Stehbens (319) and Natterson (325) both suggest help for parents in order to enable them to do "grief work" while the child still lives in order to reduce trauma.

The emotions of the dying person have been examined in detail by Elisabeth Kubler Ross in her ground-breaking book *On Death and Dying* (280). She describes five distinct stages every dying person has to go through. (1) Denial—the patient refuses to accept the diagnosis. The family can help by being patient and willing to talk. (2) Anger—anger at the unfairness of it all and envy of those more fortunate denote the beginning of the acceptance of reality. Family and friends should be understanding and not return anger. (3) Bargaining—a form of imagined thinking, that hopes that "being good" will bring reprieve. Family should show forbearance, listen, and not brush off the "bargaining." (4) Depression—the patient grieves and mourns approaching death. Family should not try to cheer the patient up; he needs to express his sorrow. (5) Acceptance—the patient has ceased to be angry or depressed. He is quietly expectant. This is the time when small talk ceases and the family's presence is all that is needed.

Of course, as Waechter (335) suggests, in order for adults to be helpful to the dying child, they must learn to accept their own feelings.

One of the most guilt-producing feelings parents of dying children experience is a secret wish that it was all over! James E. Anthony (301) comments that this is the result of the stress caused by living through a transitional stage and that there is a need for "ritualization" in order to make it bearable. Part of this ritualization has to be an endeavor to make the child's days meaningful and as normal as possible (294, 312, 322).

Parents and other family members can often benefit from therapeutic support or group therapy, where they meet with other families undergoing similar grief situations (292, 293, 311, 316, 317, 325). Futterman and Hoffman (313) suggest that if parents, after the loss of a child are able to reorganize their self-concepts, they may gain new insights, new outlooks, and new strengths.

BIBLIOGRAPHY

Books and Pamphlets for Adults

263. Anthony, James E., and Koupernik, Cyrille. *The Child in His Family: The Impact of Disease and Death.* Yearbook of the International Association for Child Psychiatry and Allied Professions. Vol. 2. New York: John Wiley & Sons, 1973.

Contains many articles by outstanding authorities on the problems of death and mourning.

264. Bernstein, Joanne E. *Helping Children Cope with Death and Separation: Resources for Teachers.* Urbana, Ill.: Publications Office/ICBD, College of Education, University of Illinois, 1976.

265. ————. *Books to Help Children Cope with Separation and Loss.* New York: R. R. Bowker, 1977.

These bibliographies are a treasury of resources of children's books, adult movies, and annotated references on research.

266. Bowlby, John. *Attachment and Loss, Volume 1. Loss, Sadness, and Depression.* New York: Basic Books, 1980.

Maintains that young children are capable of mourning, although the conditions in which they are cared for can mitigate their distress.

267. Comer, James P., and Poussaint, Alvin F. *Black Child Care: How to Bring up a Healthy Black Child in America.* New York: Pocket Books, 1975.

Written in question-and-answer form, it gives understanding advice on talking about death.

268. Easson, William M. *The Dying Child; The Management of the Child or Adolescent Who Is Dying.* Chicago, Ill.: Charles C Thomas, 1970.

Sensitive and practical book that is helpful to parents and professionals alike.

269. Fassler, Joan. *Helping Children Cope: Mastering Stress Through Books and Stories.* New York: The Free Press, 1978.

Presents the use of children's literature as a help in coping with stressful experiences. Chapter on death contains a review of children's books and a bibliography for adults.

270. Fraiberg, Selma H. *The Magic Years: Understanding and Handling the Problems of Early Childhood.* New York: Charles Scribner's Sons, 1959.

This early childhood classic contains Freudian and Piagetian insights to help parents and teachers to understand the way children feel and think.

271. Furman, Erna A. *A Child's Parent Dies: Studies in Childhood Bereavement.* New Haven: Yale University Press, 1974.

This intensive study of bereavement, contains many case histories as well as general discussion.

272. Ginott, Haim G. *Between Parent and Child: New Solutions to Old Problems.* New York: Macmillan, 1965.

Offers many concrete suggestions that will help parents to determine their children's feelings and presents appropriate ways to respond.

273. Green, Betty Radley, and Irish, D. P. *Death Education: Preparation for Living.* Cambridge, Mass.: Schenkman Publishing Company, 1971.

Makes a very good case for abandoning the taboo of pretending there is no such thing as death. This book is more interesting than depressing.

274. Grollman, Earl A. *Explaining Death to Children.* Boston: Beacon Press, 1967.

Contains two chapters filled with information focused on the younger child and his concerns.

275. ———. *Talking About Death: A Dialogue Between Parent and Child.* Boston: Beacon, 1970, 1976.

While somewhat too advanced for young children, this book might be helpful to adults who want to talk to children about death.

276. Hendrick, Joanne. *The Whole Child: New Trends in Early Education.* 2d ed. St. Louis, Mo.: The C. V. Mosby Company, 1980.

Discusses the teacher's role both in helping children to understand death and in helping the child and the family when death occurs.

277. Kellerman, Jonathan. *Helping the Fearful Child: A Guide to Everyday and Problem Anxieties.* New York: W. W. Norton, 1981.

Helpful answers to problems of parents faced with children's fears and anxieties. Provides clear distinction between "normal" fears and those that indicate need for professional help.

278. Kliman, Gilbert. *Psychological Emergencies of Childhood.* New York: Grune & Stratton, 1968.

Chapter on "Death in the Family" discusses factors that make preventive intervention desirable.

279. Krementz, Jill. *How It Feels When a Parent Dies.* New York: Alfred A. Knopf, 1981.

Presents a collection of statements of children aged 7 to 16 who have suffered the loss of a parent.

280. Kubler-Ross, Elisabeth. *On Death and Dying.* New York: Macmillan, 1976.

Shows the need for intelligent recognition of death and openness in dealing with it. Classic description of emotions of the dying person.

281. LeShan, Eda. *Learning to Say Good-Bye: When a Parent Dies.* New York: Macmillan, 1976.

This book addresses children directly—but speaks to adults too. It will be reassuring for young school-agers to read that their feelings are not unique and that they now have to allow recovery to take place.

282. Lonetto, Richard. *Children's Conception of Death.* New York: Springer, 1980.

This book, based on research with children aged 3–13, gives an insightful and candid look at thoughts children have about death. Includes sections on the fatally ill child and on childhood bereavement. Offers guidelines for adults for use in talking with children, based on the intellectual and emotional maturity of the child.

283. Mitchell, Marjorie E. *The Child's Attitude Toward Death*. New York: Schocken Books, 1967.

Presents the child's view of death, his feelings and thoughts at different ages.

284. Murphy, Lois B., and Leeper, Ethel M. *Preparing for Change*. DHEW Publication OCK 73-1028. Washington, D.C.: Department of Health, Education, and Welfare, 1973.

Discusses the feelings of young children who experience death and the resulting behaviors.

285. Murphy, Lois Barclay, and Moriarty, Alice E. *Vulnerability, Coping, and Growth from Infancy to Adolescence*. New Haven, Conn.: Yale University Press, 1976.

Examines children's personal resilience and vulnerability.

286. National Institute of Mental Health (NIMH). *Caring About Kids: Talking to Children About Death*. No. 017-024-00949-1. Washington, D.C.: Superintendent of Documents, 1979.

Sympathetic discussion that should be helpful to adults who want to discuss death with children at various developmental levels.

287. Nieburg, Herbert A., and Fischer, Arlene. *Pet Loss: A Thoughtful Guide for Adults and Children*. New York: Harper & Row, 1982.

Discusses feelings of pet owners (adults and children) connected with separation, death and losing a pet.

288. Ramos, Suzanne. *Teaching Your Child to Cope with Crisis*. New York: David McKay Company, 1975.

Presents the views of many authorities on the subject of helping children to deal with the crisis of death.

289. Rudolph, Marguerita. *Should the Children Know? Encounters with Death in the Lives of Children*. New York: Schocken Books, 1978.

Describes children's response to death based on first-hand records.

290. Sahler, Olle Jane Z., ed. *The Child and Death.* St. Louis, Mo.: The C. V. Mosby Company, 1978.

This collection of articles covers death in its many aspects as it touches the lives of children and those around them. It includes discussions of the child's concept of death, helping the family, the effects of parent suicide, helping the child who is dying, grieving for grandparents, and much more. It is a comprehensive, useful book that deals truthfully with a painful subject.

291. Schiff, Harriet Sarnoff. *The Bereaved Parent.* New York: Penguin Books, 1977.

Written by a bereaved parent this book offers suggestions and guidelines that will help parents to cope with their grief.

292. Schoenberg, Bernard; Carr, Arthur C.; Kutscher, Austin H.; Peretz, David; and Goldberg, Ivan K. *Anticipatory Grief.* New York: Columbia University Press, 1974.

States that those who have time to anticipate the death of themselves or of others are better able to cope with the reality when it comes.

293. Schulman, Anne Shaaker. *Absorbed in Living, Children Learn.* Washington, D.C.: National Association for the Education of Young Children, 1967.

Describes the way a young child was helped to accept the death of her father through nursery school experiences.

294. Spinetta, John J.; Deasy, Patricia M.; Koenig, Harold M.; Lightsey, Alton Z.; Schwartz, Donald B.; Hartman, Gary A.; and Kung, Faith H. *Talking with Children with a Life-Threatening Illness: A Handbook for the Health Care Professionals.* ERIC Document Reproduction Service, ED 178 213, 1979.

The objective of this booklet is to enable the child to live as normal a life as possible in spite of the illness.

295. Sweetland, Sandra, and Calhoun, Nancy. *Helping Children Cope with Death.* ERIC Document Reproduction Service, ED 190 977, 1980.

Written for school support personnel, this booklet offers help to those who want to help children to deal with death.

296. Wilkenfeld, Loren, ed. *When Children Die.* Dubuque, Iowa: Kendall/Hunt, 1977.

Collection of articles examining aspects of children's death.

297. Winnicott, Donald W. *The Piggle.* New York: International Universities Press, 1977.

Presents the psychoanalytic treatment of a little girl, in the course of which the analyst prepares her for his own death.

298. Wolf, Anna M. *Helping Your Child Understand Death.* Rev. ed. New York: The Child Study Press, 1973.

Provides an excellent resource for parents. It is written in question-and-answer form and is matter-of-fact and sensible.

299. Wolff, Sula. *Children Under Stress.* Rev. ed. Baltimore, Md., Penguin Books, 1973.

Suggests that children's ability to deal with bereavement depends to a large extent on the emotional reactions of the surviving parent.

300. Zeligs, Rose. *Children's Experience with Death.* Springfield, Ill.: Charles C Thomas, 1974.

Discusses children's understanding of death as they mature, their fears connected with death and the special needs of the dying child.

Studies and Articles

301. Anthony, E. James. "Editorial Comment on 'Dying.'" In *The Child in His Family: The Impact of Disease and Death,* edited by E. James Anthony and Cyrille Koupernik. Yearbook of the International Association for Child Psychiatry and Allied Professions, pp. 99–104, Vol. 2. New York: John Wiley & Sons, 1973.

Discusses the maladjustment experienced by those undergoing the process of dying and those connected with it as the outcome of a transitional stage that needs to be ritualized and routinized to be bearable.

302. Barnes, Marion J. "Reactions to the Death of a Mother." *Psychoanalytic Study of the Child* 19 (1964:334-357.

Description of the reactions of two little girls aged two and four to the death of their mother and ways in which they and their family were supported.

303. Bernstein, Joanne E. "Helping Young Children Cope with Death." In *Current Topics in Early Childhood Education*, ed. by Lillian G. Katz, pp. 179-189. Vol. 1. Norwood, N.J.: Ablex Publishing Corp., 1977.

Description of the bibliotherapy approach in coping with bereavement.

304. Bowlby, John. "Process of Mourning." *International Journal of Psychoanalysis* 42 (1961):317-340.

Describes children's mourning in three stages: protest, despair, and denial.

305. ——, and Parkes, C. Murray. "Separation and Loss Within the Family." In *The International Yearbook for Child Psychiatry and Allied Disciplines*, edited by E. James Anthony and Cyrille Koupernik. Vol. 1: *The Child in His Family*, pp. 197-216. New York: John Wiley & Sons, 1970.

Finds that young children can overcome loss only if they are helped to face their feelings and if they form a substitute relationship.

306. Brown, Nancy S.; Curry, Nancy E.; and Tittnich, Ethel. "How Groups of Children Deal with Common Stress Through Play." In *Play: The Child Strives Toward Self-Realization*, edited by Georgianna Engstrom, pp. 26-38. Washington, D.C.: National Association for the Education of Young Children, 1971.

Describes the way children were helped to deal with the experience of having witnessed a fatal accident.

307. Butler, Annie L. "Tender Topics: Children and Crises." ERIC Document Reproduction Service, ED 147 019, 1977.

Discusses children's responses to stressful events, feelings about and reactions to death and other separations. Age differences in reactions to these crises are described and discussed in terms of general cognitive development and developmental stages. Suggests that adults can help children with crisis situations by providing accurate information, encouraging the expression of feelings and by managing their own feelings and attitudes toward these same events. Ways in which outside supportive services, teachers, initial family relationships, and family life education can affect the child's responses to a crisis situation are also described.

308. Cain, Albert C.; Fast, Irene; and Erickson, Mary E. "Children's Disturbed Reactions to the Death of a Sibling." In *When Children Die*, edited by Loren Wilkenfeld, pp. 84-97. Dubuque, Iowa: Kendall/Hunt, 1977.

Discusses a wide range of enduring symptoms and distortions of character structure stemming from the death of a sibling.

309. Corr, Charles A. "Workshops on Children and Death." *Essence: Issues in the Study of Aging, Dying, and Death* 4 (1980):5-18.

Describes day-long workshops, aimed at teachers and educators, caregivers, counselors, and parents, focusing on the needs that children have in dealing with death and giving specific methods and resources.

310. Delisle, Roger G., and McNamee, Abigail S. Woods. "Children's Perceptions of Death: A Look at the Appropriateness of Selective Picture Books." *Death Education* 5 (1981):1-13.

A review of children's exposure to and perceptions of death suggests that adults might facilitate the development of children's understanding by selecting materials that present death in an age-appropriate manner.

311. Fischoff, J., and O'Brien, N. "After the Child Dies." *Journal of Pediatrics* 88 (1976):140-146.

Open-ended parent group meetings organized by parents provided mutual support through the long process of working through their grief.

312. Furman, Erna. "Helping Children Cope with Death." *Young Children* 33 (1978):25–32.

Discusses developmental stages in children's understanding of and reaction to death. Helpful guide for parents and teachers.

313. Futterman, Edward H., and Hoffman, Irwin. "Crisis Adaptation in the Families of Fatally Ill Children." In *The Child in His Family: The Impact of Disease and Death*, edited by James Anthony and Cyrille Koupernik. Yearbook of the International Association for Child Psychiatry and Allied Professions, pp. 127–143. Vol. 2. New York: John Wiley & Sons, 1973.

A dying child produces a prolonged crisis for his parents. If parents are able to reorganize their self-concepts they may gain new insights, new outlooks, and new strengths.

314. Galen, Harlene. "A Matter of Life and Death." *Young Children* 27 (1972):351–356.

Helpful guide for preschool teachers who have to deal with death.

315. Giaquinta, Barbara. "Helping Families Face the Crisis of Cancer." *American Journal of Nursing*, October 1977, pp. 1585–1588.

Describes the impact of cancer on the family as a unit.

316. Gyulay, Jo-Ellen. "The Forgotten Grievers." *American Journal of Nursing*, September 1975, pp. 1675–1679.

Describes the grief reactions of fathers, siblings, grandparents and others to terminal illness of a child.

317. Jensen, Gordon, and Wallace, John G. "Family Mourning Process." In *When Children Die*, edited by Loren Wilkenfeld, pp. 98–106. Dubuque, Iowa: Kendall/Hunt, 1977.

Urges professionals to treat family bereavement as a crisis that affects family interaction rather than a disease that affects the individual.

318. Koocher, Gerald. "Why Isn't the Gerbil Moving Any More?" *Children Today*, January 1975.

Helpful suggestions for parents and teachers on avoiding mental health problems.

319. Lascari, Andre D., and Stebbens, James A. "The Reactions of Families to Childhood Leukemia: An Evaluation of a Program of Emotional Management." *Children Pediatrics* 12 (1973):210–214.

    Describes a program for parents of children with leukemia designed to minimize their emotional problems and provide support.

320. Lonetto, Richard. "How Do Dead People Get into Heaven if They're Buried." *Essence: Issues in the Study of Aging, Dying, and Death* 4 (1980):33–45.

    Summarizes some of the major areas of concern in the study of the child's relationship with, and awareness of, death. An explanation of the changes in the child's conception is presented.

321. Major, Mike. "Helping the Bereaved Child." *Day Care and Early Education* 7 (1980):48–50.

    Discusses various approaches, some of which are more helpful to children than others.

322. Martinson, Ida M.; Geis, Dorothy; Anglim, Mary Ann; Peterson, Evelyn; Nesbit, Mark; and Kersey, John. "When the Patient Is Dying: Home care for the Child." *American Journal of Nursing*, November 1977, pp. 1815–1817.

    Reports economic and psychological benefits to both parents and children when dying children are cared for at home.

323. McDonald, Marjorie. "Helping Children to Understand Death: An Experience with Death in a Nursery School." *Journal of Nursery Education* 19 (1963):19–25.

    Describes how teachers and parents helped children to face the death of the mother of one of their classmates.

324. Nagera, Humberto. "Children's Reactions to the Death of Important Objects: A Developmental Approach." *Psychoanalytic Study of the Child*, pp. 360–399. Vol. 25. New York: International Universities Press, 1970.

Disagrees with Bowlby and others that children can mourn in the adult sense. The loss for children is a "developmental interference" that makes them create idealized fantasy parents. Children develop, depending on their developmental stage, reactions that seem similar to neurotic symptoms.

325. Natterson, Joseph M. "The Fear of Death in Fatally Ill Children and Their Parents." In *The Child in His Family: The Impact of Disease and Death*, edited by E. James Anthony and Cyrille Koupernik. Yearbook of the International Association for Child Psychiatry and Allied Professions Vol. 2. pp. 121-125. New York: John Wiley & Sons, 1973.

Suggests that extended trauma in parents can be reduced if they have an opportunity to do "grief work" while the child still lives. The therapist working with the child should focus on helping the patient to live more fully and creatively.

326. Nolfi, Mary W. "Family in Grief: The Question of Casework Intervention." In *When Children Die*, edited by Loren Wilkenfeld, pp. 75-83. Dubuque, Iowa: Kendall/Hunt, 1977.

Analyzes the paternal responses and sibling grief of five families and concludes that they would have benefitted from casework support.

327. Parness, Estelle. "Effects of Experiences with Loss and Death Among Preschool Children." *Children Today*, November/December 1975, pp. 2-7.

Examines children's stressful behavior caused by loss or separation. Suggestions for adults.

328. Phillips, Shelley. "The Child's Concept of Death: Unit for Child Studies. Selected Papers Number 8." ERIC Document Reproduction Service, ED 204 036, 1980.

Found that children under five years of age view death as reversible and not final and may believe that the dead can breathe, feel, talk, and continue to grow. However, separation by death is a painful experience for them. At the age of five, children become very curious about death and may believe that they and other children do not die. By seven or eight years of age, children begin to develop a realistic concept of death and come to terms with their own mortality. Bereaved children may commit anti-social acts, be depressed or become extremely good. They should be helped to regain feelings of security through love and acceptance and the assistance of a substitute comforter.

329. Rutter, Michael. "Separation Experiences: A New Look at an Old Topic." *The Journal of Pediatrics* 95 (1980):147–154.

Pleads for a more differentiated look at separations, considering children's age, temperament, and previous experiences.

330. Shambaugh, Benjamin. "A Study of Loss Reactions in a Seven-Year-Old." *The Psychoanalytic Study of the Child*, pp. 510–522. Vol. 16. New York: International Universities Press, 1961.

Describes the differences in grief reaction between adults and children.

331. Sheer, Barbara. "Help for Parents in a Difficult Job: Broaching the Subject of Death." *American Journal of Maternal Child Nursing*, September/October 1977, pp. 320–324.

Traces development stages in the child's concept of death.

332. Slobodzian, Kurt A., and Antes, Sally E. "Dealing with Death." *Childhood Education* 57 (1981):289–292.

Suggests that children must learn that death is "the summary of life." Urges firsthand experiences, as with the death of a small pet.

333. Stein, Myron; Beyer, Evelyn; and Ronald Doris. "Beyond Benevolence: The Mental Health Role of the Preschool Teacher." *Young Children* 30 (1975):358–372.

Argues for an increased mental health role for the preschool teacher at a time when parents might be overwhelmed by their problems.

334. Vernick, Joel. "Meaningful Communication with the Fatally Ill Child." In *The Child in His Family: The Impact of Disease and Death*, edited by E. James Anthony and Cyrille Koupernik. Yearbook of the International Association for Child Pksychiatry and Allied Professions, Vol. 2, pp. 105–119. New York: John Wiley & Sons, 1973.

Suggests that communication with children should fol-

low their concerns and interests, and that children be
offered constant opportunities to talk about everything
that will benefit them no matter how difficult for the
adult.

335. Waechter, Eugenia H. "Children's Awareness of Fatal Illness." In *When Children Die,* edited by Loren Wilkenfeld,
pp. 22–29. Dubuque, Iowa, 1977.

Discusses the various emotions of the dying child,
alienation, hostility, anxiety, and guilt. Suggests that adults
who wish to be helpful must accept their own feelings.

Books for Children

336. Aliki. *The Two of Them.* New York: Greenwillow, 1979.

Sensitive exploration of the meaning of getting old and
dying.

337. Aronson, Judith, and Heifetz, Julie. *Jodie's Present.* Clayton,
Mo.: National Cancer Society, Missouri Division, 1980.

Describes feelings and physical reactions of a child with
leukemia realistically and sensitively.

338. Bartoli, Jennifer. *Nonna.* New York: Harvey House, 1975.

Presents the experience of two children whose grandmother dies. Natural presentation that includes their participation at the funeral and the division of household
furnishings. This book can help clear up half-understood
facts about life and death.

339. Bernstein, Joanne E., and Gullo, Stephen V. *When People
Die.* New York: Atheneum, 1977.

Non-fiction book dealing with the aging process, health,
and sickness and customs of various cultures. Common
grief patterns show the universality and acceptability of
deep feelings.

340. Brown, Margaret Wise. *The Dead Bird.* 1958. Reprint. Reading, Mass.: Addison Wesley, 1965.

Simple honest presentation of death, as children experience it and accept it.

341. Carrick, Carol. *The Accident.* New York: Seabury Press,
1976.

Depicts the feelings of a boy whose dog is killed with sensitivity and a ring of authenticity.

342. ———. *The Foundling*. New York: Seabury Press, 1977.

Is it disloyal to choose a new pet when a beloved pet had died? This book explores a child's feelings in a warm, sensitive manner.

343. De Bruyn, Monica G. *The Beaver Who Wouldn't Die*. Chicago: Follett, 1975.

Beaver wishes to live forever, but finds that eternal life does not lead to happiness.

344. Dobrin, Arnold. *Scat*. New York: Four Winds, 1971.

Emphasizes the personal nature of grief and the right of each individual to deal with it in his own way.

345. Farber, Norma. *How Does It Feel to Be Old?* New York: Dutton, 1979.

Caring, realistic facing of old age and death.

346. Fassler, Joan. *My Grandpa Died Today*. New York: Behavioral Publications, 1971.

Deals with acceptance of death, feelings of loss and recovery from grief.

347. Fine, Polly Delson. *Let's Remember Corky*. University Heights, Ohio: Glickson/Stephenson, 1981.

Describes in words and photographs how a family coped with the death of their dog. Includes a special section with guidelines for helping children with loss through death.

348. Hammond, Janice M. *When My Mommy Died*. Ann Arbor, Mich.: Cranbrook, 1980.

Emphasizes the need for understanding emotions children may feel including guilt and anger. Extensive section for adults that will help them to communicate with children during a period of very great stress and help them to avoid erroneous notions.

349. Hazen, Nancy. *Grownups Cry Too/Los Adultos Tambien Lloran*. Chapel Hill, N.C.: Lollipop Power, 1973.

Accepts honest expression of emotion as appropriate. Written in English and Spanish.

350. Kantrowitz, Mildred. *When Violet Died*. New York: Parents Press, 1973.

Describes the funeral ceremony children conduct for a dead bird.

351. Kraus, Robert. *Owliver*. New York: Windmill, 1974.

Owliver's daydreams include that of the death of his parents.

352. LeShan, Eda. *Learning to Say Good-Bye: When a Parent Dies.* New York: Macmillan, 1976.

This book addresses children directly—but speaks to adults, too. It will be reassuring for young school-agers to read that their feelings are not unique and that they now have to allow recovery to take place.

353. Miles, Miska. *Annie and the Old One*. Boston: Little, Brown, 1971.

Describes the acceptance of impending death to a Navajo grandmother, and her granddaughter's struggle to accept the inescapable.

354. Ness, Evaline. *Sam, Bangs and Moonshine*. New York: Holt, Rinehart & Winston, 1966.

A father helps a young girl to finally accept the fact that her mother is dead.

355. Simon, Norma. *We Remember Philip*. Chicago: Albert Whiteman, 1979.

A group of children help their teacher whose son was killed in an accident.

356. Sonneborn, Ruth. *I Love Gram*. New York: Viking, 1971.

Centers on the imminent possibility of a beloved grandmother dying.

357. Stein, Sara Bonnett. *About Dying: An Open Family Book for Parents and Children Together*. New York: Walker, 1974.

Dual narrative, one for children, the other for the parent, is helpful in dealing with questions involving death with sensitivity and openness. Written in consultation with the staff of the Center for Preventive Psychiatry.

358. Viorst, Judith. *The Tenth Good Thing About Barney*. New York: Atheneum, 1971.

Describes a boy's sadness at the death of his pet cat and the ways he comes to terms with his feelings.

359. Warburg, Sandol. *Growing Time*. Boston: Houghton Mifflin, 1969.

Sensitive treatment of the death of an old family pet and of the emotions his parting evokes.

360. Zolotov, Charlotte. *My Grandson Lew*. New York: Harper & Row, 1974.

Depicts the fond remembrance of a grandparent.

361. ———. *If You Listen*. New York: Harper & Row, 1980.

"A little girl misses her father. He has been gone a long time." This warm book suggests ways of remembering and recalling love.

CHILDREN AND DIVORCE

"Divorce rate is a problem, reconstituted families are a problem, and growing up in every decade is becoming a more complicated business," says Dr. E. James Anthony, president of the American Academy of Child Psychiatry in a *New York Times* interview.*

Kenneth Keniston (380) found in 1977 that 33 percent of all marriages in the United States ended in divorce. His statistics probably failed to include separation and desertion, the poor man's way of ending an unsatisfactory marriage.

Almost 70 percent of divorcing couples are parents of minors, says Anthony (398); one child in seven has parents who have divorced legally.

Fassler (371) points out that since many parents who enter second marriages divorce again, children are often exposed to repeated experiences of separation and loss.

Factors discussed in the section on "Separation" enter into the consideration of the effect of divorce upon young children.

The fact that young children, especially those below three years of age, need a constant, reliable "significant adult" underlies the recommendation of Goldstein, Freud, and Solnit (375) that the "psychological parent" be given unconditional custody, including the right of denying access to the noncustodial parent. Kadushin (417) disagrees with this position. Parental responsi-

*Maya Pines, "Children of Divorce Grow up Vowing 'Same Thing Won't Happen to Me.'" *New York Times,* 13 April 1982, p. C1.

71

bilities continue, he points out, after divorce. Weakening the noncustodial parents' rights will also diminish their sense of responsibility.

Time was when children were automatically awarded to their mother by the divorce courts, unless she was considered to be "unfit." In recent years courts became increasingly aware of the fact that men can be as nurturant as women (375, 383, 400, 425, 431, 436). The possibility of living with father is even depicted in some children's books (452, 468). Santrock (436) found children living with the same sex parent better adjusted. Similar findings are reported by Tooley (442).

Steinman (441) discusses a trend that seems to gain popularity: joint custody. She found the arrangement satisfying to those adults who entered into it. Children, on the other hand, had more mixed responses.

All in all, there seems no really satisfactory solution to a problem that denotes failure and rejection to adults and evokes feelings of anger, sadness, loss, fear, guilt, and a sense of being rejected in children.

Turner (443) in an article entitled "Staying or Splitting: What's Best for the Kids," examines the available options: (1) staying together "for the children's sake," (2) a "rebuilt" marriage, (3) divorcing with "blame's the game," or (4) a "victimless" divorce. Parents, well aware of the pain that divorce can inflict, usually consider Turner's first option "staying together 'for the children's sake.'"

Many authors warn against such a decision. Rutter (434) found that much of children's disturbance following divorce was caused by the discord preceding the breakup. Despert (369) speaks of "emotional divorce" during the period preceding divorce and feels that divorce will improve rather than worsen a difficult situation for children. Children's awareness of a parental discord has even entered books for children as exemplified by Eloise Greenfield's *Talk About Family* (455). Similar conclusions are reached by Cantor (403) in her description of a play produced by third graders that shows clearly children's awareness of marital disharmony.

Parents suffering from their own pain and from the suffering caused to their children often develop feelings of anger and hostility toward their former spouses. This is not only understandable but probably a necessary component of the emotional separation they need to accomplish. But children cannot be expected to separate from one of their parents in the same way. If they get caught betwixt their parents their feelings get even more confused and unhappy. Arnstein (364), for instance, wonders whether the child, wanting to love both parents, doesn't feel guilty knowing that one wants him to hate the other. Jacobson (413) reports that children's adjustment after divorce is directly related to the amount of hostility between parents.

The tug and pull between parents can affect children's feelings about themselves as boys and girls and about the relationship between men and women. Girls may grow up thinking all men are villains; boys may become afraid to become men. Conversely, if children identify with their fathers they might reject women in general. Hetherington et al. (411) found that post-divorce effects were often more enduring among boys than among girls. Santrock and Warshak (436) found children living with the same-sex parent better adjusted. Hetherington (408, 409, 410, 411) and Wallerstein (394, 444, 445) both spent many years in studying the effects of marital separation on children. Both agree on the difficulties children undergo and suggest therapeutic intervention to help adults and children alike. Similar suggestions are made by many others (398, 416, 428, 429, 442).

Many authors (378, 385, 411, 422, 427, 428, 430, 438, 439, 440, 446) suggest that the school, and especially the preschool, can play a helpful role and provide a supportive adult to children whose parents are going through a very difficult time themselves.

Other writers (365, 368, 373, 376, 377, 378, 381, 389, 396) suggest ways parents and children can communicate. Children, sensing that their feelings, even their bad feelings of anger, fear of abandonment, and rejection are acknowledged and accepted, will find it easier to come to terms with the inevitable. It will also help them, we hope, to sort out reality and fantasy. Too often children blame themselves and their misbehaviors for their parents' going away. Other children indulge in fantasies of re-uniting their parents. Others, still, feel that somehow they must "make up" to their remaining parent and attempt to fill the role of the missing parent.

A number of authors (373, 376, 377, 458, 469) have written books with the express purpose of opening the doors of communication between parent and child. Books included in the bibliography for children in this section can also serve the purpose of helping children to see that their feelings are not unusual. Adults reading such books with children, be it parent, teacher, or another grown-up friend, should encourage open discussion.

Once divorce, or at least separation, has been accomplished, a number of secondary problems are bound to arise.

The role of the noncustodial parent is discussed by many authors (365, 391, 397, 402, 409, 413, 414, 417, 426, 447) and has entered the plots of books for children (457). The effect of financial hardships and greater mobility is discussed by Hodges (412) and Jenkins (416).

And finally, a good number of parents remarry, as described in a number of articles and books for adults and children (366, 416, 435, 458, 462, 466, 472, 474). Becoming part of a "reconstituted family" brings its own satisfactions and also problems of divided loyalties and the possibility of a new marital discord.

Most authors agree that divorce has many reasons. Certainly, since society accepted divorce as a viable solution, the number of divorces has skyrocketed. Psychologists remind us, however, that unhappy marriages are not a preferred alternative to divorce.

Sociologists look at the nuclear family, bereft of support of extended kinship connections and wonder whether the pressures young couples have to endure are not too demanding. In the meantime young people experiment with new forms and relationships that make members of the older generation very uneasy.

We ought to remember, though, that the nuclear family is a recent development and that changing ways of living will, we hope, produce solutions that fit the times and protect the children as well.

BIBLIOGRAPHY

Books and Pamphlets for Adults

362. Adams, Margaret. *Single Blessedness: Observations on the Single Status in a Married Society.* New York: Basic Books, 1976.

    Without being defensive in tone, this is a sound book that makes a good case for remaining single. It is particularly valuable for women to read who are panicky following divorce, feeling that unless they marry again, life is not worth living.

363. Akmakjian, Hiag. *The Natural Way to Raise a Healthy Child.* New York: Praeger, 1975.

    Discusses aspects of divorce that affect children including "best" time for divorce.

364. Arnstein, Helen S. *What to Tell Your Child About Birth, Illness, Death, Divorce and Other Family Crises.* New York: Condor Publishing Company, 1978.

    Discusses, in a helpful manner, various contingencies that can occur during separation and thereafter.

365. Atkins, E., and Rubin, E. *Part-Time Father: A Guide for the Divorced Father.* New York: Vanguard Press, 1976.

    A useful self-help book that discusses feelings and gives suggestions that will help to maintain a sound relationship with one's children.

366. Berman, Claire. *Making It as a Stepparent: New Roles, New Rules.* Garden City, N.Y.: Doubleday, 1980.

    Based on interviews with men and women who are stepparents, this book examines the many practical and emotional issues that are likely to crop up. While offering no ready solutions, the book will help readers to consider possible alternative resolutions in their own problem areas.

367. Blaine, Graham Burt, Jr. *Are Parents Bad for Children?* New York: Coward, McCann, 1973.

Analyzes needs of various age levels in chapter "The Effect upon Children of Divorce and Separation." Emphasizes child's need for continuing relationship.

368. Comer, James P., and Poussaint, Alvin F. *Black Child Care: How to Bring up a Healthy Black Child in America.* New York: Pocket Books, 1975.

Written in question-and-answer form, it gives understanding advice on talking about divorce.

369. Despert, Louise J. *Children of Divorce.* Garden City, N.Y.: Dolphin, 1962.

Emphasizes that the period preceding legal divorce has a great impact upon the child. Feels that divorce can improve a difficult situation for children.

370. Erikson, Erik Hamburger. *Childhood and Society.* 2d ed. New York: Norton, 1963.

Presents the basic reinterpretation of psychoanalytic theory. Explains the dynamics of attachment and "letting go."

371. Fassler, Joan. *Helping Children Cope: Mastering Stress Through Books and Stories.* New York: The Free Press, 1978.

Recommends books from contemporary children's literature that can help children cope with crises.

372. Fraiberg, Selma. *Every Child's Birthright—In Defense of Mothering.* New York: Basic Books, 1977.

Gives an eloquent description of the dynamics of parent-child attachment and of the needs of young children.

373. Gardner, Richard A. *The Parents Book About Divorce.* Garden City, N.Y., 1977.

Offers realistic guidance to parents before, during and after divorce. Helps parents to understand and deal with children's reactions.

374. Gettleman, Susan, and Markowitz, Janet. *The Courage to Divorce.* New York: Simon & Schuster, 1974.

Attempts to dispel fears that children are permanently damaged by divorce. Emphasis on opportunity for increased personal growth for all.

375. Goldstein, Joseph; Freud, Anna; and Solnit, Albert J. *Beyond the Best Interests of the Child*. New York: The Free Press, 1973.

Suggests the "least detrimental alternative" as criterion for custody, stressing the importance of the "psychological parent." They advocate fast decisions and unconditional placement, giving the custodial parent the option to determine visitation rights, if any.

376. Grollman, Earl, ed. *Explaining Divorce to Children*. Boston: Beacon Press, 1969.

Contains helpful articles on explaining divorce and the effect divorce may have on children.

377. ———. *Talking About Divorce. A Dialogue Between Parent and Child*. Boston: Beacon Press, 1975.

Facilitates discussion between parents and children.

378. Hendrick, Joanne. *The Whole Child: New Trends in Early Education*. 2d ed. St. Louis, Mo.: The C. V. Mosby Company, 1980.

Discusses many issues that arise when parents of a child in school separate.

379. Howard, A. Eugene. *The American Family: Myth and Reality*. Washington, D.C.: National Association for the Education of Young Children, 1980.

Emphasizes connectedness as the essence of family, even as family forms change with societal changes.

380. Keniston, Kenneth, and The Carnegie Council on Children. *All Our Children: The American Family Under Pressure*. New York: Harcourt Brace Jovanovich, 1977.

Presents a sweeping survey of the American family in context of the total society. Argues for a "national family policy."

381. Kliman, Gilbert. *Psychological Emergencies of Childhood*. New York: Grune & Stratton, 1968.

Discusses young children's reaction to their parents' divorce and offers helpful suggestions.

382. Kranzler, Mel. *Creative Divorce*. Philadelphia, Pa.: M. Evans & Company, 1974.

Children's reactions to divorce. Describes children's need to "mourn." Provides useful ideas on improving relationships. Positive, hopeful outlook.

383. Levine, James A. *Who Will Raise the Children? New Options for Fathers (and Mothers)*. Philadelphia, Pa.: Lippincott, 1976.

Presents the option too often overlooked: the father as the best choice as custodial parent.

384. Mindey, C. *The Divorced Mother: A Guide to Readjustment*. New York: McGraw-Hill, 1969.

Written by a divorced mother, this book does talk about children but also offers a host of practical suggestions about all aspects of life as a divorced person.

385. Murphy, Lois B., and Leeper, Ethel M. *Preparing for Change*. DHEW Publication OCD 73-1028. Washington, D.C.: U.S. Department of Health, Education, and Welfare, 1973.

Shows how the steady affection and support of the teacher can help children whose parents are separating.

386. Ramos, Suzanne. *Teaching Your Child to Cope with Crisis*. New York: David McKay, 1975.

Written primarily for parents, it cites the advice of many authorities for dealing with an assortment of crises.

387. Rofes, Eric, ed. *The Kids' Book of Divorce: By, For and About Kids*. Lexington, Mass.: Lewis Publishing Company, 1981.

This surprisingly sophisticated collection of essays written by 20 11–14 year old youngsters gives an enlightening view of divorce as seen and experienced by children.

388. Roman, Mel, and Haddad, William. *The Disposable Parent: The Case for Joint Custody*. New York: Holt, Rinehart & Winston, 1978.

Challenges current custody practices as damaging to all involved.

389. Salk, Lee. *What Every Child Would Like Parents to Know About Divorce.* New York: Warner Books, 1978.

Provides straightforward explanations, simply stated that explain the uncertainties and problems of adults and children.

390. Sell, Kenneth D. *Divorce in the Seventies: A Subject Guide to Books, Articles, Dissertations, Government Documents and Films on Divorce in the United States.* Salisbury, N.C.: Department of Sociology, Onyx Press, Catawba College, 1977.

Comprehensive bibliography.

391. Silver, Gerald A., and Silver, Myrna. *Weekend Fathers.* Los Angeles, Calif.: Stradford Press (distributed by Harper & Row, N.Y.), 1981.

Gives divorced fathers sympathy and advice on how to improve their present situation.

392. Stuart, Irving R., and Abt, Lawrence Edwin. *Children of Separation and Divorce: Management and Treatment.* New York: Van Nostrand Reinhold, 1981.

Explores a variety of issues related to the management and treatment of children affected by separation or divorce.

393. Troyer, Warner. *Divorced Kids: Children of Divorce Speak Out and Give Advice to Mothers, Fathers, Lovers, Stepparents, Brothers, and Sisters.* New York: Harcourt, Brace & World, 1979.

Written by a divorced father of eight children, it presents a look through the eyes of children at problems that may arise between non-custodial parents and their children.

394. Wallerstein, Judith S., and Kelly, Joan Berlin. *Surviving the Breakup: How Children of Parents Cope with Divorce.* New York: Basic Books, 1980.

Comprehensive view of effects of divorce based on a longitudinal research project.

395. Wheeler, Michael. *Divided Children: A Legal Guide for Divorcing Parents.* New York: W. W. Norton, 1980.

Presents a number of issues divorcing parents may want to consider.

396. Wolff, Sula. *Children Under Stress.* Rev. ed. Baltimore, Md.: Penguin Books, 1973.

Surveys children's reactions to stressful situations and suggests age-appropriate handling.

Studies and Articles

397. Ahrons, Constance R. "The Continuing Coparental Relationship Between Divorced Spouses." *American Journal of Orthopsychiatry* 51 (1981):415–428.

Found that the majority of parents continued to interact and that frequency of interaction usually went together with a more cooperative and supportive coparenting relation.

398. Anthony, James. "Children at Risk from Divorce: A Review." In *The Child in His Family: Children at Psychiatric Risk,* edited by E. J. Anthony and C. Koupernik, pp. 461–477. Yearbook of the International Association for Child Psychology and Allied Professionals. Vol. 3. New York: John Wiley, 1974.

Offers the preventive psychiatric approach to helping youngsters over the stress of divorce.

399. Baden, Clifford. "Children and Divorce: An Overview of Recent Research." ERIC Document Reproduction Service, ED 202 578, 1980.

The effects of divorce on children are the subject of this collection of eight papers by authors from several disciplines. The central theme of Albert Solnit's paper is that divorce means dissolution of the family as well as the marriage. The effects of divorce on the relationship between the child and the noncustodial parent are examined in Judith Wallerstein's study. Adolescents' reactions are discussed by Lora Heims Tessman. Urie Bronfenbrenner discusses current developments in the structure and status of the American family. A longitudinal study of the effects of divorce on the social and cognitive development of children is presented by E. Mavis Hetherington. Robert S. Weiss examines the organizational changes of divorced single-parent households and the consequences of these changes for children. The effects of child care involvement on the lifestyles of young divorced men are explored by Harry Deshet and Kristine M. Rosenthal. Finally, in a report by Nicholas Zill, the discrepancy between the clinical perspective and the findings of many field studies concerning the effects of marital conflict and divorce on children is analyzed using the results of a national survey of children.

400. Bartz, Karen W., and Witcher, Wayne C. "When Father Gets Custody." *Children Today* 7 (1978):2–6.

Discusses issues that arise when father gets custody after divorce; practical arrangements, adjustment by children and other social relationships.

401. Bentley, Eloise. "Children and Broken Homes: Sources for the Teachers." ERIC Document Reproduction Service, ED 128 735, 1975.

Urges teachers to create an atmosphere that will prevent children from divorced homes from feeling inferior to their classmates from two-parent families.

402. Butler, Annie L. "Tender Topics: Children and Crises." ERIC Document Reproduction Service, ED 147 019, 1977.

Children's responses to stressful events are discussed, such as feelings about and reactions to divorce. Age differences in reactions to these crises and other separations are described and discussed in terms of general cognitive development and developmental stages. Suggests that adults can help children cope with crisis situations by providing accurate information, by encouraging the expression of feelings and by managing their own feelings and attitudes toward these same events. Ways in which outside supportive services, teachers, initial family relationships and family life education can affect the child's responses to a crisis situation are also described.

403. Cantor, Dorothy W. "Divorce: A View from the Children." *Journal of Divorce* 2 (1979):357–361.

Presents a play written by a third-grade boy that dispels the notion that children are unaware of marital disharmony and shows the impact of divorce on children.

404. Crossman, Sharyn M., and Adams, Gerald R. "Divorce, Single Parenting, and Child Development." *Journal of Psychology* 106 (1980): 205-217.

Investigates whether a preschool intervention program for children from single-parent households could be effective in establishing the conditions appropriate for allowing the child to recover from the harmful consequences of divorce and limited adult-child interaction.

405. Gardner, Richard A. "Children of Divorce: Some Legal and Psychological Considerations." *Journal of Clinical Child Psychology* 6 (1977):3-6.

Considers that children are more vulnerable to divorce the younger they are.

406. Herzog, Elizabeth, and Sudia, Cecilia E. "Children in Fatherless Families." In *Review of Child Development Research*, edited by Bettye M. Caldwell and Henry Ricciuti, pp. 141-232. Vol. 3. Chicago: University of Chicago Press, 1973.

Focuses mainly on the single-parent family headed by the mother. But this comprehensive review touches on all problems of children living with only one parent.

407. Hess, Robert, and Camara, Kathleen. "Post-Divorce Family Relationships as Mediating Factors in the Consequences of Divorce on Children." *Journal of Social Issues* 35 (1979): 79-96.

Found that the negative effects of divorce were greatly mitigated when positive relationships with both parents were maintained after separation.

408. Hetherington, E. Mavis; Cox, Martha; and Cox, Roger. "The Aftermath of Divorce." In *Mother/Child, Father/Child Relationships*, edited by Joseph H. Stevens and Marilyn Mathews, pp. 149-176. Washington, D.C.: National Association for the Education of Young Children, 1978.

Presents a realistic look at the problems and stresses adults face, especially the first year following divorce. While marked improvement was observed thereafter, the article urges the development of support systems for the divorced family.

409. Hetherington, E. Mavis. "Family Interaction and Social, Emotional, and Cognitive Development of Children Following Divorce." Paper presented at the Symposium on the Family: Setting Priorities. ERIC Document Reproduction Service, ED 156 328, 1978.

Examines family interaction following divorce. Found that in the two years after separation the custodial parent gains in importance. However, noncustodial fathers who maintained contact had more impact than those who were detached.

410. ———. "Divorce: A Child's Perspective." *American Psychologist* 34 (1979):851–858.

Summarizes research on negative effect of divorce on children. Urges focus on how positive family functioning and support systems can further healthy development in children.

411. ———; Cox, Martha; and Cox, Roger. "Play and Social Interaction in Children Following Divorce." *Journal of Social Issues* 35 (1979):26–49.

Compared middle-class preschool children from divorced and non-divorced families. Found that while post-divorce effects are present in all, they are more enduring among boys.

412. Hodges, William F.; Wechsler, Ralph C.; and Ballantine, Constance. "Divorce and the Preschool Child: Cumulative Stress." *Journal of Divorce* 3 (1979):55–66.

Found that factors such as younger parents, geographic mobility and limited finances were more likely to cause maladjustment in preschool children of divorced families than in those from intact families.

413. Jacobson, Doris S. "The Impact of Marital Separation/ Divorce on Children: Parent-Child Separation and Adjustment." *Journal of Divorce* 11 (1978):341–360.

Examines the association between the child's psychological and social adjustment and the amount of time spent with each parent after separation.

414. ———. "The Impact of Marital Separation/Divorce on Children." *Journal of Divorce* 11 (1978):3–19.

Found that children's adjustment in the first years after divorce is directly related to the amount of hostility between parents the child was exposed to.

415. ———. "The Impact of Marital Separation/Divorce on Children. III. Parent-Child Communication and Child Adjustment and Regression Analysis from Overall Study." *Journal of Divorce* 11 (1978):175–194.

Reports on parent-child communication in connection with preparation of children for parental separation.

416. Jenkins, Shirley. "Children of Divorce." *Children Today* 7 (March/April 1978):16. (Also in *Annual Progress in Child Psychiatry and Child Development*, edited by Stella Chess and Alexander Thomas. New York: Brunner/Mazel, 1979.)

Examines the increasing number of children involved in divorce and emphasizes economic problems, custody issues, emotional problems, and changing kinship patterns of reconstituted families.

417. Kadushin, Alfred. "Beyond the Best Interests of the Child: An Essay Review." *Social Service Review* 48 (1974):508–516.

In discussing the work of Goldstein et al. (375) contends that the child's rights must be considered in context and that responsibilities of parents will be diminished if their rights are weakened.

418. Kalter, Neil, and Rembar, James. "The Significance of a Child's Age at the Time of Parental Divorce." *American Journal of Orthopsychiatry* 51 (1981):85–100.

Found that difficulties experienced in latency are often due to parental divorce during toddler years, while divorce in preschool years often led to difficulties in adolescence.

419. Kanoy, Korrel, and Miller, Brent C. "Children's Impact on the Parental Decision to Divorce." *Family Relations* 29 (1980):309–325.

Finds that children's potential for creating stress between spouses may sometimes make divorce more likely. Suggests that counseling may provide alternatives.

420. Kelly, Joan Berlin, and Wallerstein, Judith S. "The Effects of Parental Divorce: Experiences of the Child in Early

Latency." *American Journal of Orthopsychiatry* 46 (1976): 20-32.

Found that most children aged 5-7 were able to deal with divorce realistically after one year.

421. ———. "Myths and Realities for Children of Divorce." *Educational Horizons* 59 (1980):34-39.

Examines several myths such as: divorce is preferable to an unhappy home; children anticipate divorce; turmoil ends with separation; and divorce damages children. Concludes that divorce initiates a prolonged and often difficult transition for children which may benefit or harm them, depending on how parents handle it.

422. ———. "Children of Divorce." *The National Elementary Principal* 54 (1979):51-58.

Provides suggestions for teachers in order to give children support during divorce-engendered stress which may affect academic performance.

423. Kurdek, Lawrence A., and Slesky, Albert E., Jr. "Divorced Single Parents' Perceptions of Child-Related Problems." *Journal of Divorce* 1 (1978):361-369.

Seventy-three divorced single parents were asked to rate the severity of a variety of child-centered problems. The problems of greatest concern involved discipline, behavior problems resulting from the separation and following the ex-spouse's visit, and the lack of an available male model.

424. Kurdek, Lawrence. "An Integrative Perspective on Children's Divorce Adjustment." *American Psychologist* 36 (1981):856-866.

Discusses child adjustment to divorce as an interaction among four components: (1) beliefs, values, and attitudes surrounding modern family life; (2) social supports that reduce stress, and stability of the postseparation environment; (3) nature of preseparation and postseparation family functioning and support systems, and (4) children's psychological capacity for handling stress.

425. Lamb, Michael E. "The Effect of Divorce on Children's Personality Development." *Journal of Divorce* 1 (1977): 163-172.

Found that there is little support for assumptions that divorce is necessarily harmful and that custody should always be awarded to mothers.

426. Lewis, Ken. "On Reducing the Child Snatching Syndrome." *Children Today* 7 (November/December 1978):19.

Describes child snatching by non-custodial parents and its effect on children. Includes a list of organizations concerned with this and other related issues.

427. Long, Sandra M. "The Changing Child in the Changing Family." In *When There Is a Crisis: Helping Children Cope with Change*, edited by Sandra M. Long and Barbara Batchelor, pp. 12–20. Washington, D.C.: National Association for the Education of Young Children, 1979.

Examines the feelings a child may experience during and after divorce and ways in which school and parents can enhance positive developments.

428. McDermott, John F. "Parental Divorce in Early Childhood." *American Journal of Psychiatry* 124 (1967):1424–1432.

Found that divorce is a major crisis for the preschool child. Urges both teachers and mental health consultants to be aware of children's need for a reliable parent substitute as a transitory support.

429. Nadeau, Judith S.; Fagan, Stephen H.; and Schunterman, Peter. "Child Custody: The Adversarial Process as a Vehicle for Clinical Services." *Children Today* 7 (November/December 1978):14.

Describes the work of a child guidance clinic that gives aid to the court in protecting children's rights. Includes extensive criteria that indicate the need for preventive or therapeutic services.

430. Palker, Patricia. "How to Deal with the Single-Parent Child in the Classroom." *Teacher* 98 (1980):50–57.

Provides teaching suggestions, publications, and associations concerned with children of divorce and separation.

431. Parke, Ross D., and O'Leary, Sandra E. "Family Interaction in the Newborn Period: Some Findings, Some Observa-

tions of Unresolved Issues." In *The Developing Individual in a Changing World, Volume II: Social and Environmental Issues,* edited by Klaus F. Riegel and John A. Meecham, pp. 653–663. The Hague: Mouton, 1976.

Found fathers as nurturant as mothers with newborn babies.

432. Pedersen, Frank A., and Robson, Kenneth S. "Father Participation in Infancy." *American Journal of Orthopsychiatry* 39 (169):466–472.

433. Rubin, Lisa D., and Price, James H. "Divorce and Its Effects on Children." *Journal of School Health* 49 (1979):552–556.

Shows stages of children's adjustment after divorce and discusses the emotional processes involved.

434. Rutter, Michael. "Parent-Child Separation: Psychological Effects on Children." *Journal of Child Psychology and Psychiatry* 12 (1971):233–260.

Found that children's delinquency following divorce was caused by the discord that preceded the breakup, rather than by the separation itself.

435. ———. "Separation Experiences: A New Look at an Old Topic." *The Journal of Pediatrics* 95 (1980):147–154.

Pleads for a more differentiated look at separations, considering children's age, temperament, and previous experiences. Some separations alter circumstances for the better. Warring parents refraining from divorce may neglect children's needs for familial harmony. Some separations indicate psychiatric risk, however.

436. Santrock, John W., and Warshak, R. A. "Father Custody and Social Development in Boys and Girls." *Journal of Social Issues* 35 (1979):112–125.

Found that children living with the same sex parent are better adjusted.

437. Seegel, Virginia F. "The Divorced Parent and the Hospitalized Child: Implications for the Hospital Staff." *Journal of the Association for the Care of Children in Hospitals,* Fall 1978, pp. 16–18.

Describes additional stresses on the single parent of the hospitalized child.

438. Schoyer, Nancy L. "Divorce and the Preschool Child." *Childhood Education* 57 (1980):2–7.

Offers help to teachers by explaining some defense behaviors children may exhibit and giving suggestions for helping.

439. Skeen, Patsy, and McKenry, Patrick G. "The Teacher's Role in Facilitating a Child's Adjustment to Divorce." *Young Children* 35 (1980):3–12.

Helps teachers to recognize and provide for the special needs children may have during the stressful time of divorce.

440. Stein, Myron; Beyer, Evelyn; and Ronald, Doris. "Beyond Benevolence: The Mental Health Role of the Preschool Teacher." *Young Children* 30 (1975):358–372.

Argues for an increased mental health role of preschool teachers at a time when parents might be overwhelmed by their problems.

441. Steinman, Susan. "The Experience of Children in a Joint Custody Arrangement: Report on a Study." *American Journal of Orthopsychiatry* 51 (1981):403–414.

Finds that joint custody was found satisfactory by parents who chose it; however, the children had more mixed responses.

442. Tooley, Kay. "Antisocial Behavior and Social Alienation Past Divorce: The Man of the House and the Mother." *American Journal of Orthopsychiatry* 46 (1976):33–42.

Describes the possible social alienation of divorced women and the resultant aggressive behavior of their sons. Family therapeutic intervention produced dramatic improvement.

443. Turner, M. C. "Staying or Splitting: What's Best for the Kids." *Journal of Family Counseling* 6 (1978):52–54.

Examines the four available options, e.g., staying together "for the children's sake," divorcing with "blame's the game," a "rebuilt" marriage, or a "victimless" divorce.

444. Wallerstein, Judith S., and Kelly, Joan Berlin. "The Effects of Parental Divorce: Experiences of the Preschool

Child." *Journal of the American Academy of Child Psychiatry* 14 (1975):600–616.

Found psychological deterioration in behavior and function of many children as well as poorer mother-child relationship. Suggests preventive measures.

445. ———. "Children and Divorce: A Review." *Social Work* 24 (1979):468–474.

Discusses the emotional impact of divorce on children and adolescents after reviewing the literature and findings. Implications for practice, research and social policy.

446. Whitfield, Edie L., and Freeland, Kent. "Divorce and Children: What Teachers Can Do." *Childhood Education* 58 (1981):88–89.

Suggests classroom activities that can be helpful to children.

447. Woolner, Rosetelle B. "'What Do We Do Today, Daddy?' Father's Perception of His Role and Responsibilities." ERIC Document Reproduction Service, ED 158 882, 1977.

Studies found that the non-custodial father accepts his legal responsibilities, wants to be more involved, and aims to serve as a model and a protector. Middle-class subjects.

448. Yarrow, Leon J. "Separation from Parents During Early Childhood." In *Review of Child Development Research*, edited by Martin L. Hoffman and Lois Wladis Hoffman, pp. 89–136. Vol. 1. New York: Russell Sage Foundation, 1964.

Summary of research analyzing factors that affect children's reactions to various separations from parents, i.e., day care, institutionalization, multiple mothering, hospitalization, maternal employment, and father separation.

Books for Children

449. Adams, Florence. *Mushy Eggs*. New York: Harcourt Brace Jovanovich, 1976.

Shows a family managing well after divorce.

450. Berger, Terry. *A Friend Can Help*. Milwaukee: Raintree, 1974.

     Tells how important it is to have a friend to share your feelings.

451. ———. *How Does It Feel When Your Parents Get Divorced?* New York: Messner, 1977.

     Questions and thoughts of a young girl may encourage children to come to terms with their own feelings.

452. Eichler, Margrit. *Martin's Father*. Chapel Hill, N.C.: Lollipop Power, 1971.

     Shows Martin being brought up by his father. The mother is not mentioned.

453. Gardner, Richard A. *The Boys and Girls Book About Divorce*. New York: Science House, 1970.

     This honest book should be helpful to older children to accept and deal with realities.

454. Goff, Beth. *Where Is Daddy? The Story of a Divorce*. Boston: Beacon Press, 1969.

     Allows children to identify with a little girl whose experiences and feelings may be similar to their own.

455. Greenfield, Eloise. *Talk About Family*. Philadelphia, Pa.: Lippincott, 1978.

     Genny is eager for her eldest brother's return from the military, convinced that he will fix the growing rift between their parents.

456. Grollman, Earl A. *Talking About Divorce: A Dialogue Between Parent and Child*. Boston: Beacon Press, 1975.

     Includes one section for children and one for parents. Reassuring for children, although somewhat Pollyannaish in assuming that deep love between parents and children always exists and continues.

457. Kindred, Wendy. *Lucky Wilma*. New York: Dial, 1973.

     Describes satisfying Saturdays a little girl spends with her father.

458. Le Shan, Eda. *What's Going to Happen to Me? When Parents Separate and Divorce*. New York: Four Winds Press, 1978.

     Filled with examples of a variety of families, this book

should be reassuring to children and helpful to adults helping them to cope.

459. Lexau, Joan. *Me Day*. New York: Dial, 1971.

Deals realistically with children's feelings and confusions about divorce, poverty, and loneliness.

460. ———. *Emily and the Klunky Baby and the Next Door Dog*. New York: Dial, 1972.

Shows how a child's feelings of resentment and need for added attention are finally resolved. Suburban setting.

461. Lisker, Sonia O., and Dean, Leigh. *Two Special Cards*. New York: Harcourt Brace Jovanovich, 1976.

After Hazel's parents divorce she wonders if father will ever come back. She realizes, however, that her father still loves her.

462. Palmer, Heidi. *I Have Two Families*. Nashville, Tenn.: Abingdon, 1981.

Shows that divorce does not have to be devastating. Patty and Michael are now living in two places!

463. Perry, Patricia, and Lynch, Marietta. *Mommy and Daddy Are Divorced*. New York: Dial Press, 1978.

Describes two boys who try to understand and cope with their parents' divorce.

464. Rogers, Helen. *Morris and His Brave Lion*. New York: McGraw-Hill, 1975.

Father gives Morris a stuffed lion to help him to be brave when he leaves the family. When father has difficulties facing his family again, Morris sends him the lion. Father and lion attend Morris' birthday party.

465. Roy, Ron. *Breakfast with My Father*. Boston: Houghton Mifflin/Clarion, 1980.

Depicts a situation where the father returns for a trial reunion.

466. Salzman, Yuri. *Where Do I Fit In?* New York: Holt, Rinehart & Winston, 1981.

When John's mother remarries he wonders where he fits in. His stepfather's parents help him regain his self-confidence.

467. Schuchman, Joan. *Two Places to Sleep*. Minneapolis: Carol-
     rhoda Books, 1979.

     Relates how a child comes to accept his parents' separa-
     tion, realizing that they will continue to love him, although
     they do not love each other.

468. Sitea, Linda. "Zachary's Divorce." In *Free to Be You and Me*,
     edited by Marlo Thomas et al., pp. 124–129. New York:
     McGraw-Hill, 1974.

     Depicts two children of divorced parents. Zachary lives
     with his mother, his friend Amy with her father.

469. Stein, Sara Bonnett. *On Divorce: An Open Family Book for
     Parents and Children Together*. New York: Walker & Com-
     pany, 1979.

     Dual narrative, one for children, the other for parents,
     is helpful in discussing divorce that will help all to deal
     with their feelings together. Written in consultation with
     the Center for Preventive Psychiatry.

470. Stenson, Janet Sinberg. *Now I Have a Stepparent and It's Kind
     of Confusing*. New York: Avon Books, 1979.

     Written to be read aloud, this book will help children to
     share and understand their conflicting emotions. Foreword
     for adults.

471. Surowiecki, S. *Joshua's Day*. Chapel Hill, N.C.: Lollipop
     Power, 1972.

     Tells about a single working mother and her son who
     attends a day care center.

472. Thomas, Ianthe. *Eliza's Daddy*. New York: Harcourt Brace
     Jovanovich, 1976.

     Shows how a little girl's feelings about her father's
     remarriage are eased by visiting his new "family." *Let Me
     Read Book*.

473. Van Leeuwen, Jean. *Too Hot for Ice Cream*. New York: Dial,
     1974.

     The main emphasis of this book is on the adventures
     and good times of two little girls. Their parents' separation
     is treated as an accepted background plot.

474. Vigna, Judith. *She's Not My Real Mother*. Chicago: Albert
     Whitman, 1980.

Describes the mixed feelings of a young boy toward his stepmother and how he comes to accept her.

475. Zolotov, Charlotte. *If You Listen*. New York: Harper & Row, 1980.

Asks "How do you know someone far away is loving you?" and gives a warm, reassuring answer.

476. ———. *A Father Like That*. New York: Harper & Row, 1971.

Depicts the daydreams of a little boy who never knew his father.

SINGLE PARENT FAMILIES

Do you remember your first readers in first grade? Dick and Jane, their baby sister Sally, their dog Spot and their cat Fluff? These children represented what publishers considered the "American" family. Dick and Jane were white, they lived in a one-family house, their mother stayed home while their father went to work with a briefcase under his arm.

There never was a single American prototype, of course. Nowadays publishers know better. See, for instance, Norman's *All Kinds of Families* (525) portraying the full gamut of American family life, including single-parent families.

In fact, even single-parent families are not uniform. There are parents who were married and are now single heads of households through divorce or death. These can be men or women. Then there are single mothers who never were married.

Kornfein, Weisner, and Martin (504) talk about three different kinds of single mothers. (1) "Nestbuilders"—usually identified with the women's movement—saw motherhood as a desirable part of the total female experience. These were usually employed, middle-class women who were competent in arranging for child care and for social activities for themselves. (2) "Post hoc adaptors" tended to be younger and less well educated than the first group. Their pregnancies usually were unwanted, sometimes carried to term in the hope of marrying the baby's father. Their employment record and their relationships with men were often unstable. Many relied on public assistance for support. Some returned to their families. (3) "Unwed mothers" tended to be younger than the first two groups—often in their teens. They usually turned to their parents for support. The maternal grandmother often took on the mothering role, while the young mother's status was somewhat ambiguous.

Eiduson (498) reports on intensive longitudinal studies of single mothers and finds a number of further interesting features.

Elective single mothers seemed to have demographic characteristics similar to their married counterparts with the possible exception of the stability of their parents' marriage. They often tended to reject traditional middle-class values and preferred alternative life styles, i.e., social contract relationships or living in groups. However, their educational and achievement aspirations for their children were similar to those of young married mothers. Most of these single mothers returned to study or work when their child was between two and three years old.

Post hoc adaptors were the least satisfied with their status. About 50 percent of this group changed their family style before the child's first birthday. They continued to experiment with different relationships and they moved more frequently than the other two groups.

Unwed mothers, being more dependent, had fewer options and moved the least often.

As a group, single mothers were not satisfied with their life. The parenting behavior of single mothers seemed more rigid, with a higher number of parent-initiated rather than child-initiated contacts and least encouragement toward independence of the child.

A number of studies and books (480, 481, 484, 494) examine the emotional state of the post-divorce and widowed single parent. These men and women have to readjust after a difficult emotional separation. Single fathers are discussed by a comparatively large number of authors (486, 488, 499, 505, 508, 510, 512) and have even found their way into books for children (522, 527, 531). Grasser (499) found that divorced fathers considered themselves better adjusted than widowers, possibly because their role was more based on their own decision. Middle-class fathers seemed more harassed and resentful than lower-class fathers.

How does growing up in a single-parent home affect children? Grow (500) found that children of single mothers were not less well adjusted than those of intact families. The effect of growing up without a father was examined by Dahl (495) who found children of long-term Vietnam prisoners less well adjusted. Biller (478) and Kurdek and Siesky (506) found that single mothers were concerned about the lack of available male models. According to Segal (489), Bach (492), and Pedersen (511), boys are more likely to be affected than girls.

Margaret Mead (507) suggests that children growing up with only one adult miss out on being able to choose between parents. They also do not experience adult conversation.

A number of authors, such as Doering (497) and Weiss (515) agree that children of single parents develop a sense of responsibility and a precocious self-reliance.

Not all authors view growing up in a single-parent household as disadvantageous. Klein (483) finds that, although single parents tend to "bend over backwards," studies do not seem to find a significant difference in the emotional make-up of their children, with the possible exception of fear of separation. Even more exhaustive is the look at research by Herzog and Sudia (502, 503). These authors reviewed 400 studies dealing with fatherless homes. They found no significant difference with regard to behavior, intellectual ability or achievement between children from fatherless homes and two-parent families.

Children's mode of experiencing their family's status depends to a large extent on the experiences they have outside the home. Not so long ago, for instance, primary grades had a social studies unit called *The Family* that discussed families of Dick and Jane, but not of any other variety. Teachers, principals, and other service personnel have to become aware that they cannot disregard alternative family life styles. Moreover, since the school provides the primary alternative experience children have with adults, the role of these adults and their awareness of the children's (and their parents') needs become even more important. The school's role is discussed by a number of authors (493, 496, 478) in this section.

A look at children's books gives us an amazingly candid view about the way children see their life, as grasped and depicted by sensitive authors. Children feel resentment (517, 521); they can feel lonely (526, 518); they develop substitute relationships (517, 523, 527, 528); they daydream about absent fathers (520, 530); they feel challenged to be the "man of the house" (524, 673); and they have some very good times (522, 525, 529, 531) under a variety of circumstances.

Single parents sometimes have a predisposition to compare their lives and the lives of their children with some mythical ideal. Since, however, such ideals are hard to come by, they might find it reassuring that the joys and sorrows, satisfactions and frustrations they and their children experience might be different, but not necessarily better or worse than the struggle of others.

BIBLIOGRAPHY

Books and Pamphlets for Adults

477. Adams, Margaret. *Single Blessedness: Observations on the Single Status in a Married Society.* New York: Basic Books, 1976.

Without being defensive this book makes a good case for remaining single.

478. Biller, Henry B. *Paternal Deprivation: Family, School, Sexuality, and Society.* Lexington, Mass.: Lexington Books, 1974.

Comprehensive review of psychological aspects of father absence.

479. Coonrod, Debbie. *Fathering: The Effect of Father-Absence and Inadequate Fathering on Children's Personality Development.* Bloomington, Ind.: Debcon, 1981. (Also available in ERIC Document Reproduction Service, ED 200 317, 1981.)

Reviews the influence of fathers and the effect of their absence or of inadequate fathering.

480. Hope, Karol, ed. *Momma: The Sourcebook for Single Mothers.* New York: New American Library, 1976.

Contains articles by and about single mothers.

481. Kamerman, Sheila B. *Parenting in an Unresponsive Society.* New York: Free Press, 1980.

Describes how women manage child care, family responsibilities, work, and other problems by using excerpts from interviews, vignettes, and daily logs.

482. Kelly, Marguerite, and Parsons, Ella S. *The Mother's Almanac.* Garden City, N.Y.: Doubleday, 1975.

While not exclusively for the single parent, this book—and also the one by S. Adams Sullivan (490) is based on interviews with dozens of fathers and mothers with different lifestyles and varying levels of experience. Practical tips including such difficult subjects as discipline and divorce.

483. Klein, Carole. *The Single Parent Experience*. New York: Avon Books, 1973.

Provides a realistic and compassionate view of the motivations, feelings, and specific problems of single parents. Although single parents often have a tendency to "bend over backward," studies show that there is no significant difference in the emotional make-up of children from one-parent homes with the possible exception of fear of separation.

484. Knight, Bryan M. *Enjoying Single Parenthood*. Toronto: Van Nostrand Reinhold, 1980.

Helps single parents to get in touch with their own feelings and to develop constructive alternatives to self-defeating behavior.

485. Levine, James E. *Who Will Raise the Children? New Options for Fathers (and Mothers)*. Philadelphia, Pa.: Lippincott, 1976.

Presents the option too often overlooked: the father as the best choice as a custodial parent.

486. McFadden, Michael. *Bachelor Fatherhood: How to Raise and Enjoy Your Children as a Single Parent*. New York: Walker & Company, 1974.

Presents a frank, positive picture of his own experiences as a bachelor father, with a good discussion of the pitfalls of bringing up a young child.

487. Rosenthal, Kristine M., and Keshet, Harry F. *Fathers Without Partners: A Study of Fathers After Marital Separation*. Totowa, N.J.: Rowman & Littlefield, 1981.

Discusses custody, joint custody, and visitation. Considers the needs of both fathers and their children.

488. Schlesinger, Benjamin. *The One-Parent Family: Perspectives and*

Annotated Bibliography. Rev. ed. Toronto, Canada: University of Toronto Press, 1978.

Review of studies on motherless families, fatherless separated families, divorce and children, widowhood, the unmarried mothers, single parent adoptions in Canada, the USA, and Australia.

489. Segal, Julius, and Yahraes, Herbert. *A Child's Journey: Forces that Shape the Lives of Our Young.* New York: McGraw-Hill, 1978.

Concludes that the absence of a father can have deleterious effects on the sense of identity of their children.

490. Sullivan, S. Adams. *The Father's Almanac.* Garden City, N.Y.: Doubleday, 1980.

Companion volume to *The Mother's Almanac*—see discussion of same under: Kelly, Marguerite, and Parsons, Ella S. (482)

491. Weiss, Robert S. *Going It Alone: The Family and Social Situation of the Single Parent.* New York: Basic Books, 1979.

Considers the social situation of the man or woman who has to care for children alone by presenting a wealth of interviews.

Studies and Articles

492. Bach, George R. "Father-Fantasies and Father-Typing in Father-Separated Children." *Child Development* 17 (1946): 63–68.

This often quoted study found that boys growing up without fathers were less aggressive, more dependent and had weaker masculine self-concepts.

493. Brown, B. Frank. "A Study of the School Needs of Children from One-Parent-Families." *Phi Delta Kappan* 61 (1980): 537–540.

Found some differences in the school behavior and achievement of children from one-parent families with increasing differences as children get older. Urges review of curriculum and school services in order to serve the needs of these children better.

494. Burgess, Jane K. "The Single-Parent Family: A Social and Sociological Problem." *The Family Coordinator* 19 (1970): 137–144.

Emphasizes that children are better off in a post-divorce, single-parent home than they were before the divorce when the family was disorganized.

495. Dahl, Barbara B., and McCubbin, Hamilton. "Prolonged Family Separation in the Military: A Longitudinal Study." In *Families in the Military System*, edited by Hamilton McCubbin and Barbara B. Dahl. Beverly Hills, Calif.: Sage Publications, 1976.

Studied children of Vietnam prisoners who were absent for several years and those whose fathers did not return. Both groups scored below norm in social and personal adjustment.

496. Damon, Parker. "When the Family Comes Apart: What Schools Can Do." *The National Elementary Principal* 59 (1979):66–75.

Describes problems of children where parents are in the process of separating and gives suggestions to teachers and principals.

497. Doering, William G. "Is Life in a One-Parent Family Damaging to Children?" ERIC Document Reproduction Service, ED 193 546, 1980.

Found children in one-parent families more independent. In all other respects there was no difference between one- and two-parent family children.

498. Eiduson, Bernice. "Contemporary Single Mothers." In *Current Topics in Early Childhood Education*, edited by Lillian G. Katz, pp. 65–76. Vol. 3. Norwood, N.J.: Ablex, 1980.

Followed up three types of single mother distinguished by Kornfein et al. (504). Found significant differences between the three groups in life-style and mother-child relationships.

499. Grasser, Rita, and Taylor, Claribel M. "Role Adjustment of Single Parent Fathers with Dependent Children." *The Family Coordinator* 25 (1976):397–401.

Found that fathers' attitudes varied depending on the cause of their present status. Divorced fathers considered themselves better adjusted than widowers.

500. Grow, Lucille J. "Early Childrearing by Young Mothers: A Research Study." ERIC Document Reproduction Service, ED 179 315, 1979.

Examined relationship between the mother's marital status at the time of the baby's birth, her age and other maternal characteristics, experiences and attitudes, and the subsequent well-being of mother and child of 440 white women under 25 years of age. Results showed that, although the unwed mothers were less educated, less enthusiastic about motherhood than their married counterparts, their marital status had no harmful impact on the development and adjustment of their children.

501. Heger, Donna Tubach. "A Supportive Service to Single Mothers and Their Children." *Children Today* 7 (September/October 1977):2.

Describes a program for young single mothers aimed at helping them to realize their capacity for self-support and independent living and for developing parenting skills.

502. Herzog, Elizabeth, and Sudia, Cecilia E. "Children in Fatherless Families." In *Review of Child Development Research*, edited by Bettye M. Caldwell and Henry N. Ricciuti, pp. 141–232. Chicago: University of Chicago Press, 1973.

Focuses mainly on the single-parent family headed by the mother. But this comprehensive review touches on all problems of children living with only one parent.

503. ———. "Fatherless Homes: A Review of Research." *Children* 15 (1968):177–182.

Reviewed close to 400 studies dealing with fatherless homes. Found that there was no significant difference in regard to behavior, intellectual ability, achievement, and emotional adjustment between children from fatherless homes and those from two-parent families.

504. Kornfein, Madeline; Weisner, Thomas S.; and Martin, Joan C. "Women into Mothers: Experimental Family

Life Styles." In *Women into Wives: The Legal and Economic Impact of Marriage*, edited by Jane Roberts Chapman and Margaret Gates, pp. 259–291. Beverly Hills, Calif.: Sage Publications, 1977.

Divided single mothers into three categories: (1) nest-builders, who saw single motherhood as desirable; (2) post hoc adaptors, who did not plan their pregnancies, but decided on having the child; (3) unwed mothers, very young women, still dependent on their own families.

505. Keshet, Harry Finkelstein, and Rosenthal, Kristine M. "Single Parent Fathers: A New Study." *Children Today* 7 (May/June 1978):13.

Of 49 fathers interviewed most expressed satisfaction in spite of problems in child rearing and managing time for both job and children.

506. Kurdek, Lawrence A., and Siesky, Albert E., Jr. "Divorced Single Parents' Perceptions of Child-Related Problems." *Journal of Divorce* 1 (1978):361–369.

Seventy-three divorced single parents were asked to rate the severity of a variety of child-centered problems. The problems of greatest concern involved discipline, behavior problems resulting from the separation and following the ex-spouse's visit, and the lack of an available male model.

507. Mead, Margaret. "Every Home Needs Two Adults." *Redbook Magazine*, May 1976. Reprinted in *Readings in Early Childhood Education* 77/78, edited by Judy Spitler McKee, pp. 167–168. Guilford, Conn.: Dushkin Publishing Group, 1977.

Contends that children in one-parent homes miss out on a sense of choice between two adults and on experiencing conversations on an adult level.

508. Mendes, Helen A. "Single Fathers." *The Family Coordinator* 25 (1976):439–444.

Interviewed middle-class single fathers and found them resentful and feeling stressed.

509. Norton, Arthur J. "A Portrait of a One-Parent Family." *The National Elementary Principal* 59 (1979):32–39.

Describes problems of children from single-parent families and gives suggestions to teachers and principals.

510. Orthner, Dennis K.; Brown, Terry; and Fergusen, Dennis. "Single Parent Fatherhood: An Emerging Family Life Style." *The Family Coordinator* 25 (1976):429–437.

Found that single-parent fathers were satisfied with their lives and successful as single parents.

511. Pedersen, Frank A.; Rubenstein, Judith L.; and Yarrow, Leon J. "Infant Development in Father-Absent Families." *Journal of Genetic Psychology* 135 (1979):51–62.

Male babies in single-parent black families measured significantly lower than average in mental development, social development and preference for novel stimuli. Female babies were not affected.

512. Schlesinger, Benjamin. "Single Parent Fathers: A Research Review." *Children Today* 7 (May/June 1978):12.

Examines studies on motherless families in four English-speaking industrialized countries.

513. Seegel, Virginia F. "The Divorced Parent and the Hospitalized Child: Implications for the Hospital Staff." *Journal of the Association for the Care of Children in Hospitals*, Fall 1978, pp. 16–18.

Describes the additional stresses experienced by single parents of a hospitalized child.

514. Weiss, Robert J. "Going It Alone." *The National Elementary Principal* 59 (1979):14–30.

Discussion on how single parents cope.

515. ———. "Growing up a Little Faster: Children in Single Parent Households." *Children Today* 10 (1981):22.

Examines the development of children in single parent households. These children have responsibilities for chores, for younger siblings and often serve as a partner to their parent in decision making. For younger children this can produce a precocious self-reliance and denial of dependence needs.

516. Woods, Merilyn B. "The Unsupervised Child of the Working Mother." *Developmental Psychology* 6 (1972):14–25.

Found that children of lower class working mothers had better social and personal adjustment if their mothers were satisfied with their work and with child-care arrangements.

Books for Children

517. Baldwin, Anne Norris. *Jenny's Revenge.* New York: Four Winds, 1974.

    Jenny resents it that her newly divorced mother goes to work and leaves her with a babysitter. Her efforts to alter the situation fail, but the babysitter's childhood memories help her to accept her new situation.

518. Clifton, Lucille. *Some of the Days of Everett Anderson.* New York: Holt, Rinehart & Winston, 1970.

    Describes feelings of loss and feelings of joy of a little boy whose father is absent and whose mother works.

519. ———. *Everett Anderson's Year.* New York: Holt, Rinehart, & Winston, 1974.

    A poem for each month describes the feelings of a little boy who lives with his mother.

520. ———. *Everett Anderson's Friend.* New York: Holt, Rinehart & Winston, 1976.

    Shows children's fantasies about absent father. Positive resolution of conflict with mother.

521. Eber, Christine. *Just Momma and Me.* Chapel Hill, N.C.: Lollipop Power, 1975.

    A young girl is not sure she likes it when her mother's boyfriend moves in.

522. Eichler, Margrit. *Martin's Father.* Chapel Hill, N.C.: Lollipop Power, 1971.

    Shows Martin being brought up by his father. The mother is not mentioned.

523. Schick, Eleanor. *City in Winter.* New York: Macmillan, 1970.

    Jimmy has fun with his grandmother while his mother works. Father is absent.

524. ———. *Neighborhood Knight.* New York: Greenwillow, 1976.

Depicts a preschooler's fantasy as a knight who protects his mother and sister.

525. Simon, Norman. *All Kinds of Families*. Chicago: Albert Whitman, 1976.

Nonfiction book that portrays the vast varieties of family life including single parents, parents in prison, large families, families who live in a circus, and those in an igloo. Emphasis is on shared joy and sadness.

526. Sonneborn, Ruth A. *The Lollipop Party*. New York: Viking, 1967.

Tomas, who lives with his working mother and sister, finds himself alone when his mother is delayed and his sister must leave.

527. Steptoe, John. *My Special Best Words*. New York: Viking, 1974.

Written in black dialect this book explores the daily life of two children, their father and their babysitter.

528. Stanek, Muriel. *I Won't Go Without a Father*. Chicago: Albert Whitman, 1972.

Shows how children can form substitute relationships with men other than their father.

529. Zindel, Paul. *I Love My Mother*. New York: Harper & Row, 1975.

Shows a single parent mother who not only cooks but teaches her son to kick a football.

530. Zolotov, Charlotte. *A Father Like That*. New York: Harper & Row, 1971.

Depicts the daydreams of a little boy who never knew his father.

531. ———. *The Summer Night*. New York: Harper & Row, 1974.

Depicts a day of a little girl cared for by her father.

CHILDREN OF WORKING MOTHERS

In the middle of the present century, the '50s and '60s, there was a fairly consistent cleavage along social lines among women. Lower-class women usually worked. Their children were often cared for by "baby-sitters," neighborhood women who looked after a few children in addition to their own baby. Sometimes day-care centers were available to the working mother.

The working middle-class mothers were the exception rather than the rule. These women often felt pangs of guilt for "neglecting" home, husband, and child. Society's message as carried by women's magazines, child-rearing books, pediatricians, and speakers at PTA meetings was fairly unanimous. Preschool children need their mothers. Mother should stay at home at least until her youngest reaches elementary school.

Nursery schools rather than day-care centers were used by the middle class if they used preschool programs at all. These programs offered shorter hours than is usual for day care. Some met only 2–3 times a week. Infant day care was unheard of. Sometimes "being toilet trained" was used as a criterion for the child's readiness for preschool. At the same time both early childhood professionals and parents were aware that in addition to the educational and emotional boons children derived from going to nursery, their mothers benefited from calling a few hours their own, and that this in turn eased family tensions, thus bringing advantages to all of its members.

Sociologists will probably tell us how the change came about in the '60s. Women's work—housework—became less demanding. Dishwashers, washing machines, refrigerators, packaged foods, vacuum cleaners, the concept of "planned obsolescence," all played their part. At the same time, as these expensive toys (including the ubiquitous automobile and TV set) became accepted as a measure of one's standard of living, many mothers drifted back to work, often picking up their premarital occupations in order to help eke out the family finances and keep up with payments—and with the Joneses.

The women's movement entered around this time emphasizing self-fulfillment and a right to a meaningful life for women. Day care suddenly was looked upon not so much as an emergency solution but a means to free women so that they could live a more meaningful life.

While the slow drift of women into the market place went comparatively unnoticed, the women's movement raised many anxieties. Conservative, social, political, and religious forces suddenly saw old-time family values endangered.

Senator Walter Mondale and Representative John Brademas drafted a Comprehensive Child Development Bill after such services were strongly recommended by the White House Conference on Children of 1970. The bill was encouraged by Richard Nixon, who was then President, and was acted upon favorably by both houses of Congress. However, forces opposing women going to work mounted such a strong letter-writing campaign that in 1971 the president vetoed the Bill. The charges leveled against the Bill were unfounded: Day care was not to be obligatory; parents would have been able to utilize the facilities if they wanted to. No woman would have been coerced into handing her child into the care of others. There were many interesting parts to this lost dream. Let me just mention three. (1) The bill provided for flexible fee scales; thus all children would have been eligible to enter centers and to remain there if the family's financial status changed either way. This flexible fee scale would have allowed for a social mix among child and parent populations. (2) The bill required parent participation in the development, operation, and evaluation of centers, thus preventing a sense of powerlessness parents may feel when they hand over part of the responsibility for their children to others. (3) While probably still insufficient, the bill provided for funding that was based on the concept of *quality* day care.

This was not to be. The bill was rewritten, resubmitted but never passed in any form that resembled the original concept.

Of course, women, as we know, continued to enter the marketplace. Lois W. Hoffman (582) presented in 1979 an update of her 1974 study (544) in which she reviews the consequences of the mother's work on herself, her husband, and her child.

Hoffman differentiates between social levels. Children of professional women, as indicated also by Hartley (579), are provided with a role model, modifying children's stereotyped expectations about women's work. (See also children's books referring to these ideas—612, 615, 617, 618, 623)

Children of lower-class mothers, as emphasized by Woods (607), have a better social and personal adjustment if their mothers are happy in their jobs and are happy about care arrangements for their children.

Hoffman finds that mothers satisfied with their work become better mothers and that mothers who feel they are self-sacrificing either by going to work or by deciding not to, provide poor mothering. Many mothers with young children report, however, that feelings of guilt mar their satisfaction with work. Family life styles have changed, according to Hoffman. Fathers participate more in the running of the home; there is greater emphasis on independence for children; family times together are more carefully planned.

Hoffman finds no research evidence that shows deleterious effects of mothers' working on school-age children, nor is there a significant increase in delinquency rates.

Shirley Moore (586) in a review of research in 1978 agrees; there is little evidence that maternal employment has a negative effect particularly where school-age children are concerned. Their scholastic achievement does not differ from those of the other children. Daughters of working mothers have higher job aspirations. On the other hand, some often have lower opinions of their fathers.

What about preschoolers?

A great proportion of the bibliography in this section deals with child care arrangements for infants and toddlers, i.e., children under 2½ or 3 and for preschoolers aged between 2½ or 3 and 5 or 6.

The factors around separation and individuation of babies are discussed in greater detail in the essay preceding the section on *Separation*. Suffice it to say here that questions were raised by Ainsworth (65), Blehar (566), Fraiberg (541), the Robertsons (595), Tyler and Dittman (603), Vaughn et al. (605), and others who were concerned about the emotional development of very young children in infant day-care and the potential weakening of the mother-child bond. These issues are far from resolved. Many studies (538, 564, 565, 570, 573, 575, 577, 580, 581, 583, 586, 587, 590, 593, 594) found no significant difference in attachment and emotional health of infants and toddlers who were in group or family day care *provided* such care was of high quality. This proviso should be taken very seriously. The studies that found positive results were usually conducted in university-based infant care centers of exceptional quality. It was usually possible for infants to form a substitute attachment to *one* caregiver (Cummings, 573; Ricciuti, 594; Egeland, 575; Gonzales, 578; Hazen, 580). That this is not always feasible under normal circumstances is described by Wilcox et al. (606).

Brazelton and his associates (569) suggest that mothers should plan to be with their infants for at least the first 3–4 months until the babies' physiological rhythms have stabilized.

Burton White (559) finds that it is far more preferable if a child under three is cared for by his mother, or if this is not possible, by a close relative. The next in order of choices should be a caregiver in the home who shares the parents' values. The next choice, according to White, should be family day care, the modern-day equivalent of the woman who "baby-sits" in her own home. Infant group care should be used only as a last resort. Kagan and his associates (584) suggest that children be enrolled in group care either between the ages of one and seven months or when they are older than fifteen to eighteen months. Since there are highly respected authorities warning against enrolling very young babies, Kagan's second alternative, i.e., above eighteen months, seems to be the wiser choice if at all possible, in view of studies on separation and individuation (550). Glickman and Springer (543) and Michael Rutter (597) urge reduced hours of attendance for infants and toddlers and suggest that mothers of infants or toddlers work half-days if that is feasible.

Advantages of preschool for children above about three years have long been demonstrated. These studies are beyond the scope of this book and are, therefore, not included. There are, however, many kinds of preschools and many qualitative and philosophical differences even among each type. For parents able to pay tuition, there are cooperative nursery schools—usually run on a nonprofit basis—with parent participation. There are various types of preschools organized by churches, temples, and synagogues, often on a nondenominational basis. Many private and independent schools for older children include preschool classes. There are experimental and laboratory schools attached to many universities. There are privately owned and franchised preschool centers. Parents considering to enroll their child would do well to visit several schools (without their child) and try to imagine their child in these surroundings. The National Association for the Education of Young Children publishes a helpful flyer: *Some Ways of Distinguishing a Good Early Childhood Program* (30¢). Write to: NAEYC, 1834 Connecticut Avenue N.W., Washington, D.C. 20009.

For children of poor parents (and for handicapped children) there are also many choices. There are prekindergartens in some public schools. These usually accept only certain children, i.e., below a certain income limit or those who are handicapped. Services provided differ in various communities. Headstart centers differ in their source of funding and often in their location, but services provided and populations served are similar to prekindergarten. Headstart services also vary from place to place. Publicly funded day care centers are set up for the "working poor" and for children of welfare parents. There is a firm family income limit. This may mean a "revolving door" policy where children cannot be retained even if this would be in their best interest.

Elizabeth Prescott in an article (591) and in a booklet (554) discusses the qualitative differences between various day-care centers and other child-rearing environments. Centers vary widely, she points out, and so do children. When children spend almost all of their waking hours away from home, the center must fulfill a great variety of needs. Preschoolers still need the anchor of one warm accepting, but firm, adult. They need opportunities to use their large muscles— to run, climb, build, slide, tug, lift, to play in sand and water, to exercise their imagination and to explore the many fascinating things this world contains. They need to test their own limits and to find out, through trial and error "how to make friends and influence people." They need to be rambunctious and they need to be quiet. But they do *not* need over-regimentation, lessons based on teacher-talk rather than hands-on experience. Preschool teachers, says Prescott, often feel that to deserve the title, they too must "teach," using the methods and curriculum of the elementary school as a model. But premature structuring and premature regimentation restricts children. It prevents them from stretching their emotional, social, and intellectual muscles.

The mother looking for a good preschool might do well to look for one that allows children to be children and to remember that young children learn by playing.

BIBLIOGRAPHY

Books and Pamphlets for Adults

532. Albrecht, Margaret. *A Complete Guide for the Working Mother.* Garden City, N.Y.: Doubleday & Company, 1967.

    Practical book that looks at realities as well as research and gives many suggestions to the working mother.

533. Beyer, Evelyn. *Teaching Young Children.* Indianapolis, Inc.: Bobbs-Merrill, 1968.

    Discusses parent-school relations that are based on mutuality.

534. Cook, Alice H. *The Working Mother: A Survey of Problems and Programs in Nine Countries.* Ithaca, N.Y.: Cornell University, 1975.

    Compared conditions of employed mothers in Sweden, Israel, East Germany, West Germany, Roumania, Austria, Russia, Japan, and Australia. Urges a "Maternal Bill of Rights."

535. Day, Mary Carol, and Parker, Ronald K., eds. *The Preschool in Action: Exploring Childhood Programs.* 2d ed. Boston: Allyn & Bacon, 1977.

    Contains an overview of a variety of preschool designs.

536. Dittman, Laura, ed. *The Infants We Care For.* Washington, D.C.: National Association for the Education of Young Children, 1973.

    A collection of papers on infant day care contributed by the NAEYC Commission on the Care and Education of Infants.

537. Dizard, J. *Social Change in the Family*. Chicago: Community and Family Study Center, University of Chicago Press, 1968.

Makes a connection between role-sharing among husbands and wives and wife-employment. Fathers' participation in child-care, child socialization, and housework can lead to greater marital happiness and better adjustment of children.

538. Evans, E. Belle, and Saia, George. *Day Care for Infants: The Case for Infant Day Care and a Practical Guide*. Boston: Beacon Press, 1972.

Makes a case for infant day care without reservations. Provides a practical guide for all aspects of establishing and running a program.

539. Edward, Joyce; Ruskin, Nathene; and Turini, Patsy. *Separation-Individuation: Theory and Application*. New York: Gardner Press, 1981.

Presents Mahler's theory of separation-individuation with illustrative case studies.

540. Fein, Greta G., and Clarke-Stewart, Alison. *Day Care in Context*. New York: John Wiley & Sons, 1973.

Offers an interpretation of child development research that can serve as a knowledge-base in developing child care that is responsive to the needs of children and their families.

541. Fraiberg, Selma. *Every Child's Birthright: In Defense of Mothering*. New York: Basic Books, 1977.

Warns against infant day care, which might damage the child's capacity for deep feeling.

542. Galinsky, Ellen, and Hooks, William H. *The New Extended Family: Day Care That Works*. Boston: Houghton Mifflin, 1977.

Describes what works and how in a variety of programs of quality across the United States including both group care and family day care.

543. Glickman, Beatrice Marden, and Springer, Nasha Bass. *Who Cares for the Baby?: Choices in Child Care*. New York: Schocken Books, 1978.

Surveys the various options for infants and toddlers and concludes that mothers of very young children should work half-days whenever possible.

544. Hoffman, Lois Wladis, and Nye, F. Ivan. *Working Mothers.* San Francisco: Jossey-Bass Publishers, 1974.

Presents an evaluative review of the consequences of mothers' work for wife, husband, and child.

545. Holmstrom, Lynda Lyttle. *The Two-Career Family.* Cambridge, Mass.: Schenkman Publishing Company, 1973.

While mentioning child-care issues, the main focus of this book is on husband-wife relationships.

546. Kagan, Jerome; Kearsley, Richard B.; and Zelazo, Philip A. *Infancy: Its Place in Human Development.* Cambridge, Mass.: Harvard University Press, 1978.

Contains the authors' report on their study on infant day-care. They found that in general infants reared at home developed similarly to day-care babies with respect to cognitive, social, and affective qualities. They suggest that children be enrolled either between the ages of one and seven months or when they are older than fifteen to eighteen months and include many other suggestions for quality day care.

547. Kahn, Alfred J., and Kamerman, Sheila B. *Child Care Programs in Nine Countries: A Report Prepared for the OECD Working Party on the Role of Women in the Economy.* Washington, D.C.: Office of Child Development, Department of Health, Education, and Welfare, 1976. Available from ERIC Document Reproduction Service, ED 121 428.

Contains comprehensive descriptions, highlights, and discussion of common problems of Canada, France, West Germany, Israel, Poland, Sweden, and the United Kingdom.

548. Kenniston, Kenneth, and the Carnegie Council on Children. *All Our Children: The American Family Under Pressure.* New York: Harcourt Brace Jovanovich, 1977.

Examines child development in context of family, community, and society. Provides extensive factual information and suggests wide-ranging social reform.

549. Lazar, Irving; Hubbel, B. R.; Murray, H.; Rosche, M.; and Royce, J. *Summary Report: The Persistence of Preschool Effects: A Long Term Follow-up of Fourteen Infant and Preschool Experiments.* OHDS 7830129. Washington, D.C.: Administration for Children, Youth, and Families, OCD, HEW, 1977.

A resounding vote of confidence for quality early childhood education.

550. Mahler, Margaret S.; Pine, Fred; and Bergman, Anni. *The Psychological Birth of the Human Infant: Symbiosis and Individuation.* New York: Basic Books, 1975.

Presents separation and individuation as complementary developmental processes as the child gradually separates from the fusion with his mother during the ages of five months and three years, by moving from autism through symbiosis to object constancy where he can retain the inner representation of his mother.

551. Norris, Gloria, and Miller, Jo Ann. *The Working Mother's Complete Handbook.* New York: E. P. Dutton & Company, 1979.

Gives a wealth of helpful suggestions and provides emotional support for working mothers.

552. Nye, Frances Ivan, and Hoffman, Lois W. *The Employed Mother in America.* Chicago: Rand McNally, 1963.

Reports studies that show more favorable attitudes toward children by working mothers than by nonworking mothers.

553. Olds, Sally Wendkos. *The Mother Who Works Outside the Home.* New York: Child Study Press, 1975.

Discusses feelings of mothers, fathers, and children and gives many practical suggestions.

554. Prescott, Elizabeth, and Jones, Elizabeth. *Day Care as a Child-Rearing Environment.* Washington, D.C.: National Association for the Education of Young Children, 1972.

Finds that day care can, under favorable circumstances,

be advantageous to young children. However, quality of day care can differ widely and individual children's needs differ also. Offers criteria for evaluating centers.

555. Provence, Sally. *The Challenge of Day Care.* New Haven, Conn.: Yale University Press, 1977.

While based on experience with high-risk infants this book contains much good advice on planning a nurturing day-care program, the human relations factors and problems dealing with separation.

556. Rice, F. Philip. *A Working Mother's Guide to Child Development.* Englewood Cliffs, N.J.: Prentice-Hall, 1979.

A wealth of information including answers to specific questions working mothers may ask.

557. Roland, Alan, and Harris, Barbara. *Career and Motherhood: Struggles for a New Identity.* New York: Human Sciences Press, 1979.

A collection of psychiatric and psycho-historical essays discussing the "dual role" of the college-educated professional woman.

558. Weissbourd, Bernice, and Musick, Judith, eds. *Infants: Their Social Environments.* Washington, D.C.: National Association for the Education of Young Children, 1981.

A collection of articles summarizing recent infant research and social development affecting babies.

559. White, Burton T. *The First Three Years of Life.* Englewood Cliffs, N.J.: Prentice-Hall, 1975.

Studies in the development of competence in young children.

560. Willis, Anne, and Ricciuti, Henry. *A Good Beginning: Guidelines for Group Day Care.* Washington, D.C.: National Association for the Education of Young Children, 1975.

Offers detailed guidelines to infant day care centers. Emphasizes that infant day care of quality should be an option available to working mothers, either full or part time, and that while the availability of such facilities is desirable, parents should be able to choose from many options.

Studies and Articles

561. Allen, Mary J., and Friedle, James. "Guilt and Anxiety in Mothers with Young Children." ERIC Document Reproduction Service, ED 208 982, 1981.

    Found that mothers with an intact marriage who were at home with their children exhibited the least amount of guilt and anxiety. Single working mothers with children in nursery school showed the most guilt and anxiety.

562. Bee, Helen L. "The Effect of Maternal Employment on the Development of the Child." In *Social Issues in Developmental Psychology*, edited by Helen L. Bee, pp. 97–106. New York: Harper & Row, 1974.

    Found that the mother's employment has no adverse effect if the family is stable.

563. Beels, C. Christian. "The Case of the Vanishing Mommy." *The New York Times Magazine*, 4 July 1976. Reprinted in *Readings in Human Development 78/79*, edited by Bradley B. Glanville and Andrew Gilpin, pp. 136–140. Guilford, Conn.: Dushkin Publishing Group, 1978.

    Discusses the change in expectations of mothers in our society, which encourages mothers to enter the job market while still expecting them to be "Madonna types."

564. Belsky, Jay, and Steinberg, Lawrence D. "The Effects of Day Care: A Critical Review." *Child Development* 49 (1978):929–949.

    Examines past studies and concludes that day care does not disrupt the mother-child bond and benefits the child's social development.

565. Blanchard, Marie, and Main, Mary. "Avoidance of the Attachment Figure and Social Emotional Adjustment in Day-Care Infants." *Developmental Psychology* 15 (1979): 445–446.

    Found that children who had spent a year in substitute care showed less avoidance behavior than cited by Blehar (566) and higher social-emotional adjustment implying that "adjustment" of infants to substitute care may not take as long as previously thought.

566. Blehar, Mary Curtis. "Anxious Attachment and Defensive

Reactions Associated with Day-Care." *Child Development* 45 (1974):683–692.

Observed separation and reunion with mothers in a strange situation of two- and three-year olds, comparing home-reared children with children who had five months of day care experience. Found that the day-care children manifested an impairment in the attachment to their mothers.

567. Boocock, Saranne S. "A Crosscultural Analysis of the Child Care System." In *Current Topics in Early Childhood Education*, ed. by Lillian G. Katz. Vol. 1, pp. 71–103. Norwood, N.J.: Ablex Publishing, 1977.

Makes comparisons between child care in the United States, Israel, and Sweden in terms of parents, caretaking, and the role of government.

568. Brazelton, T. Berry. "Working with the Family." In *The Infants We Care For*, edited by Laura Dittman, pp. 17–29. Washington, D.C.: National Association for the Education of Young Children, 1973.

Warns that in a stressful environment parents may abdicate the psychological care of their children if their self image is poor. Centers must take care not to load the negative side of parental ambivalence by making parents feel ineffective.

569. ———; Koslowski, Barbara; and Main, Mary. "The Origins of Reciprocity: The Early Mother-Infant Interaction." In *The Effect of the Infant on the Caregiver*, edited by Michael Lewis and Leonard A. Rosenblum, pp. 49–76. New York: John Wiley & Sons, 1974.

Suggests that mothers should plan to be with their babies for at least three or four months until the infant's physiological rhythms have stabilized.

570. Caldwell, Bettye M.; Wright, Charlene M.; Honig, Alice S.; and Tannenbaum, Jordan. "Infant Day Care and Attachment." *American Journal of Orthopsychiatry* 40 (1970):397–412.

Found no difference in mother-child attachment between toddlers in an infant day care center and those reared at home.

571. Cohen, Sarale E. "Maternal Employment and Mother-Child Interaction." *Merrill-Palmer Quarterly* 24 (1978):189–197.

Found that mothers and children were less attentive to each other when mothers worked.

572. Cornelius, Steven W., and Denney, Nancy Wadsworth. "Dependency in Day Care and Home Care Children." *Developmental Psychology* 11 (1975):575–582.

Found no difference in measures of dependency between home-reared and day-care five year olds. Day-care girls were more independent and differed less from boys than home-reared girls.

573. Cummings, E. Mark. "Caregiver Stability and Day Care." *Developmental Psychology* 16 (1980):31–37.

Toddlers showed no distress and seemed to form an immediate attachment to the caregiver in a day care center if the caregiver remained stable and her schedule and that of the child coincided.

574. Dittman, Laura L. "Where Have All the Mothers Gone and What Difference Does It Make?" In *Infants: Their Social Environments*, edited by Bernice Weissbourd and Judith Musick, pp. 129–145. Washington, D.C.: National Association for the Education of Young Children, 1981.

Emphasizes that babies need a primary caregiver who establishes a reciprocal relationship, where the personalities of the infant and caregiver become attuned to each other. Urges recognition and financial reward of caregiving as a profession.

575. Egeland, Byron, and Sroufe, L. Alan. "Attachment and Early Maltreatment." *Child Development* 52 (1981):44–52.

Found that infants were attached to their caretakers even if mistreated.

576. Etaugh, Claire. "Effects of Maternal Employment on Children: A Review of Recent Research." *Merrill-Palmer Quarterly* 20 (1974):71–98.

Reviewed the literature comparing preschool children attending group care with home-raised children. Found no significant ill effect, such as anxiety, feeding problems, bed wetting, over-dependence, or antisocial behavior, that would signal ill-effects of group care.

577. Farran, Dale C., and Ramey, Craig T. "Infant Day Care and Attachment Behavior Toward Mothers and Teachers." *Child Development* 48 (1977):1112–1116.

Found that toddlers of low socioeconomic status who were cared for in day-care centers beginning with 2–3 months overwhelmingly preferred their mothers to their teachers.

578. Gonzales-Mena, Janet. "What Is a Good Beginning?" *Young Children* 34 (1979):47–51.

Infants, the author maintains, need more than mere stimulation. They need "synchrony"—harmonious or reciprocal interaction, the give-and-take of a partnership or team.

579. Hartley, Ruth E. "What Aspects of Child Behavior Should Be Studied in Relation to Maternal Employment?" In *Research Issues Related to Effects of Maternal Employment and Children*, edited by A. E. Spiegel. University Park, Pa.: Social Science Research Center, 1961.

Found that maternal employment affects children's concepts of the female role.

580. Hazen, N. "The Effects of Day Care on Infants and Toddlers." In *Review of Research for Practitioners and Parents*. University of Minnesota, 1978.

Found that infants and toddlers can form secure attachments to center caregivers and that group care is not harmful provided center quality is high and adult child ratio is three or four children per adult.

581. Hock, Ellen. "Working and Nonworking Mothers with Infants: Perception of Their Careers, Their Infants' Needs, and Satisfaction with Mothering." *Developmental Psychology* 14 (1978):37–43.

Working mothers perceived less infant distress at separation and were less anxious about separation and about the care givers. There was no difference between working and nonworking mothers in maternal satisfaction and in career orientation.

582. Hoffman, Lois Wladis. "Maternal Employment: 1979." *American Psychologist* 34 (1979):859–865.

In this update of the earlier study (544) it was found that (1) there is a difference between families who use day care and those who do not; (2) fathers tend to take a more active role in family life if the mother works; (3) working improves the mother's self-esteem; (4) there is a different interaction style between mothers and children when mothers work.

583. Jordan, Ruth. *A Commitment to Children: The Report of the Labor Union Women Child Care Seminar, Sponsored by the German Marshall Fund of the United States.* Detroit: Coalition of Labor Union Women, 1977. ERIC Document Reproduction Service, ED 153 709.

Describes a visit of seminar members who examined child-care provisions from the point of view of working women in Sweden, France, and Israel.

584. Kagan, Jerome; Kearsley, Richard B.; and Zelazo, Philip A. "The Effects of Infant Day Care on Psychological Development." *Evaluation Quarterly* 1 (1977):104–142.

Found that if infants are cared for in well-run centers it does no harm to their development.

585. Kanter, Rosabeth Moss. "Jobs and Families." *Children Today* 7 (March/April 1978):11.

Discusses a variety of job-related factors that affect family life, such as timing of shifts and of free time; job-related rewards, i.e., money and prestige; cultures within occupations, such as white- and blue-collar work; and the emotional climate of work.

586. Moore, Shirley G. "Working Mothers and Their Children." *Young Children* 34 (1978):77–82.

Offers a review of research comparing children of working mothers with home-reared children. Although the data are still sparse, there is no evidence of ill effect provided the group or family day care is of high quality.

587. Moscowitz, Debbie S.; Schwarz, Conrad J.; and Corsini, David A. "Initiating Day Care at Three Years of Age: Effects on Attachment." *Child Development* 48 (1977): 1271–1276.

Found that children with day-care experience were not impaired in their mother attachment in a situation similar to that used by Blehar (566).

588. Newberry, Phyllis; Weissman, Myrna M.; and Myers, Jerome K. "Working Wives and Housewives: Do They Differ in Mental Status and Social Adjustment?" *American Journal of Orthopsychiatry* 49 (1979):282–291.

Working women were found to derive much more satisfaction and enjoyment from their work than housewives.

589. Olds, Sally Wendkos. "When Mommy Goes to Work." *Family Health/Today's Health*, February 1977, pp. 38–40.

Examines the effects mothers' working outside the home has on children. Offers guidelines for parents that help to avoid emotional difficulties.

590. Portnoy, Fern, and Simmons, Carolyn H. "Day Care and Attachment." *Child Development* 49 (1978):239–242.

Compared home-reared children, children who entered day care at age 3, and children who entered day care at 3 after two years of family day care experience. Found no significant differences in attachment patterns.

591. Prescott, Elizabeth. "Is Day Care as Good as a Good Home?" *Young Children* 33 (1978):13–19.

Takes a critical look at day care centers and generally finds them inferior to Head Start, cooperative nurseries, or good family day care. Suggests less regimentation, variable adult-child ratio with opportunity for individualization and centers not larger than 60 children.

592. Ragozin, Arlene S. "Attachment Behavior of Day Care Children: Naturalistic and Laboratory Observations." *Child Development* 51 (1980):409–415.

Found that day care for middle-class children aged

17-38 months was compatible with normal attachment behavior.

593. Ramey, Craig T. "Consequences of Infant Day Care." In *Infants: Their Social Environments*, edited by Bernice Weissbourd and Judith Musick, pp. 65-76. Washington, D.C.: National Association for the Education of Young Children, 1981.

    Finds that children can be cared for in group care beginning with early infancy without adverse effects on their health or their attachment to their parents and with possible intellectual benefits, provided that the day care is of high quality.

594. Ricciuti, Henry N. "Fear and the Development of Social Attachments." In *The Origins of Fear*, edited by Michael Lewis and Leonard A. Rosenblum. New York: John Wiley & Sons, 1974.

    Found that infants and toddlers did form an attachment with one center caregiver while the mother/child attachment remained intact. Centers investigated were of high quality with special emphasis on caregiver stability.

595. Robertson, James, and Robertson, Joyce. "Taking the Side of Under-Threes." *Australian Women's Weekly*, 20 July 1977.

    Feel that day care for very young children weakens the mother/child bond.

596. Roopnarine, Jaipaul L., and Lamb, Michael E. "The Effects of Day Care on Attachment and Exploratory Behavior in a Strange Situation." *Merrill-Palmer Quarterly* 24 (1979):85-95.

    Found that while three year olds about to enter day care were more anxious than home-care children, the differences disappeared three months later.

597. Rutter, Michael. "Separation Experiences: A New Look at an Old Topic." *The Journal of Pediatrics* 95 (1980):147-154.

    Pleads for a more differentiated look at separations, considering children's age, temperament, and previous experiences. Mothers' refraining from work may neglect children's needs for familial harmony.

598. ———. "Social-Emotional Consequences of Day Care for Preschool Children." *American Journal of Orthopsychiatry* 5 (1981):4–28.

Discusses social and emotional results of day care for toddlers or preschool children. Urges quality care and reduced hours, especially for toddlers.

599. Schacter, Frances Fuchs. "Toddlers with Employed Mothers." *Child Development* 52 (1981):958–964.

Compared children of employed and non-employed mothers and found no difference in emotional adjustment. However, the children of employed mothers were more peer-oriented and self-sufficient and less jealous than those of non-employed mothers.

600. Schwarz, J. Conrad; Strickland, Robert G.; and Krolik, George. "Infant Day Care: Behavioral Effects at Preschool Age." *Developmental Psychology* 10 (1974):502–506.

Children with previous infant day care experience were found more verbally aggressive, less cooperative, more active, and less tolerant of frustration than their peers.

601. Seegmiller, Bonni R. "Effects of Maternal Employment on Sex-Role Differentiation in Preschoolers." ERIC Document Reproduction Service, ED 175 579, 1979.

Found that the fact of the mother's working and the social status of her occupation were unrelated to sex-role differentiation.

602. Sulby, Arnold, and Diodati, Anthony. "Family Day Care: No Longer Day Care's Neglected Child." *Young Children* 30 (1975):239–247.

Describes a family day care program in a large Eastern city.

603. Tyler, Bonnie, and Dittman, Laura L. "Metting the Toddler More than Halfway: The Behavior of Toddlers and Their Caregivers." *Young Children* 35 (1980):39–46.

Compared toddlers reared at home or in family day care with those in group center care. Center children showed more self-comforting behavior and used less speech. Home children evinced a greater range of emotional expression.

604. Vandell, Deborah Lowe. "Effects of a Playgroup Experience on Mother-Son and Father-Son Interaction." *Developmental Psychology* 15 (1979):379–385.

   Compared toddlers in a playgroup to totally home-reared children. Playgroup toddlers became more active in interacting with their parents and responsive to their parents' initiative. Parents of playgroup children became less dominant.

605. Vaughn, Brian E.; Gore, Frederick L.; and Egeland, Byron. "The Relationship Between Out-of-Home Care and the Quality of Infant-Mother Attachment in an Economically Disadvantaged Population." *Child Development* 51 (1980):1203–1214.

   Infants receiving day care were found to show more anxious and avoiding behavior when meeting strangers.

606. Wilcox, Barbara Morgan; Staff, Phyllis; and Romaine, Michael F. "A Comparison of Individual with Multiple Assignment of Caregivers to Infants in Day Care." *Merrill-Palmer Quarterly* 26 (1980):53–62.

   Found it impossible to provide one stable caregiver for infants. They were cared for by a group of five providers who were familiar with the babies.

607. Woods, Merilyn B. "The Unsupervised Child of the Working Mother." *Developmental Psychology* 6 (1972):14–25.

   Found that children of lower-class working mothers had better social and personal adjustment if their mothers were satisfied with their work and with child care arrangements.

608. Wortis, Rochelle Paul. "The Acceptance of the Concept of the Maternal Role by Behavioral Scientists: Its Effects on Women." *American Journal of Orthopsychiatry* 41 (1971):733–746.

   Examines the prevailing assumption that the primary caregiver of a child must be the natural mother and urges alternative possibilities.

609. Yarrow, Leon J. "Separation from Parents During Early Childhood." In *Review of Child Development Research*, ed. by

Martin L. Hoffman and Lois Wladis Hoffman, pp. 89–
136. Vol. 1. New York: Russell Sage Foundation, 1964.

Summary of research analyzing factors that affect children's reactions to various separations from parents, i.e., day care, institutionalization, maternal employment, and father separation.

610. Yarrow, Marian Radke; Scott, Phyllis; De Leeuw, Louise; and Heinig, Christian. "Childrearing in Families of Working and Nonworking Mothers." *Sociometry* 25 (1962): 122–140.

Found that the mother's satisfaction with her work contributes to family stability.

611. Zambana, Ruth E.; Hurst, Marsha; and Hite, Rodney L. "The Working Mother in Contemporary Perspective: A Review of the Literature." *Pediatrics* 64 (1979):862–868.

Provides an overview of research which should help teachers and other professionals who counsel working mothers and their families.

Books for Children

612. Bauer, Caroline Feller. *My Mom Travels a Lot*. New York: Frederick Warne, 1981.

While mom is away on business, dad holds the fort as well as he can.

613. Blaine, Margaret. *The Terrible Thing That Happened at Our House*. New York: Parents Magazine Press, 1975.

Describes the reaction of children when their mother returns to work after several years at home.

614. Clifton, Lucille. *Everett Anderson's Year*. New York: Holt, Rinehart, & Winston, 1974.

Everett is an elementary school age "latchkey child." The book describes his feeling and fantasies.

615. Heyman, Abigail. *Butcher, Baker, Cabinetmaker: Photographs of Women at Work*. New York: Thomas Y. Crowell, 1978.

This non-fiction book should go a long way to destroy sex stereotypes.

616. Hill, Elizabeth S. *Evans Corner*. New York: Holt, Rinehart, & Winston, 1967.

     Adam attends a day care center, while both his parents work.

617. Lasker, Joe. *Mothers Can Do Anything*. Chicago: Albert Whitman, 1972.

     Shows mothers in various occupations, including high administrative positions, plumbers, and dentists.

618. Merriam, Eve. *Mommies at Work*. New York: Scholastic, 1961.

     Describes "all kind of mommies at all kinds of jobs."

619. Schick, Eleanor. *City in the Winter*. New York: Macmillan, 1970.

     Depicts a very special grandmother who cares for Jimmy while mother is at work.

620. ———. *Home Alone*. New York: Dial, 1980.

     Andy is home alone under the watchful eye of a neighbor while his mother is at work. An Easy-to-Read book.

621. Smith, Lucia B. *My Mom Got a Job*. New York: Holt, Rinehart & Winston, 1979.

     A family shares responsibilities when mother goes to work.

622. Sonneborn, Ruth. *The Lollipop Party*. New York: Viking, 1967.

     Tomas is taken to the day care center by his mother and is picked up by his sister. His teacher and his cat are important and comforting parts of his life.

623. Vestley, Ann-Cath. *Hello Aurora*. New York: Thomas Y. Crowell, 1974.

     A young girl and her father do all the chores, while mother, an attorney, is at work.

SIBLING RELATIONS

A priest once happened upon two young boys fighting bitterly. "Why do you fight each other?" he asked. "Don't you know that we should love our enemies?"

"He is not my enemy," panted one of the boys. "He is my brother."

In our concern about "bad" feelings we sometimes overlook the real feelings of kinship that exist between brothers and sister. Usually the good and bad feelings exist side by side, resulting in ambivalence that confounds neat classifications (624, 626). These mixed feelings are illustrated even in some books for children (683, 702, 708).

Of course, apart from individual differences and environmental variables (642) we have to consider a number of additional factors.

Anna Freud (627) and David Elkind (653) consider the effect of the child's developmental level. Freud in her stage-by-stage description of the child's development indicates that at first children are too egocentric to consider siblings as anything but rivals for the love of their parents. In the next stage other children (siblings or peers) are seen much like lifeless objects which can be manipulated without expecting positive or negative responses from them. After that, toddler age children accept their siblings into the home community, but they prefer acting as helpmates to them, be it playing, building, destroying, causing mischief, or anything else. Only toward the end of the preschool period are other children considered people in their own right, who can be admired, feared, competed with, loved, or hated. The child begins to identify feelings of others, acknowledge and often respect their wishes and possibly even share possessions on a basis of equality.

Elkind considered the development of the concept "brother" and found three stages: non-differentiated, concretely differentiated, and abstract concepts. The concept of "having a brother" also has three stages: asymmetrical, intuitively symmetrical, and abstractly symmetrical. The ability to comprehend the nature of the relationship, says Elkind, affects the relationship itself.

A large proportion of the literature considers the feelings of the first-born, who overnight loses "top billing" (624, 625, 626, 680, 710). A reassuring book for children by Ann H. Scott (700) repeats what mothers have been telling their children for ages, that there is "room for two on mother's lap." Psychologists find, however, that mothers' feelings *do* change after the second child arrives. Dunn and Kendrick (651) found that mothers gave their firstborn less attention after the birth of the baby and that confrontations between mother and oldest increased, partly because the child's behavior had changed. At the same time others found that mothers' relations to the firstborn remained different from those to their subsequent children. Firstborn children were more dependent and their mothers more interfering and inconsistent with them according to Hilton (656). Jacobs and Moss found that mothers spent less time with the new baby than with the older child (657).

Some psychologists consider this unequal time distribution all to the good. They describe the older child's feeling of rejection, "wasn't I good enough?" (624, 626), their need for extra love and reassurance (624, 626), their anger, jealousy, resentment (626), and the feeling of being left out (629).

Children's behavior can change radically after a baby's arrival. Children often become more babyish (624, 680); either they regress as a response to stress, or they imitate the baby, endeavoring to regain their lost position. Children who were toilet trained suddenly start soiling and wetting again. Thumbs pop back into mouths, children ask to be bottlefed again, and they give up their independence, becoming clinging and "baby-ish."

Some children who had adjusted well to preschool suddenly refuse to go as they realize that their mother stays home making time with baby. This is most certainly not a good time to *start* nursery school. Children are likely to interpret this as being kicked out of the nest.

If preschool is well established in the child's life, it can play a helpful role by allowing the child to work out his mixed-up feelings (629, 632, 635).

Preschool can be the steady thread in the child's life while mother is in hospital. It can provide for opportunities to "play baby" while emphasizing that this is only pretend. *Real* babies never, never go to school! It also allows children to play mother occasionally giving the doll-babies the treatment they know they can't inflict on the live one. Children's anger can bubble out in play with their age mates, under the watchful eye of the teacher, who does not let things go too far lest they increase feelings of guilt even further. Some children, on the other hand, may show sadness and lethargy. Schools often use books about new babies (676–710) at story periods, giving reassurance to the child that his feelings are not unique.

Stories can serve a useful purpose at home, too (626, 701), providing for opportunities to talk about and accept feelings. It is important for children to know that their feelings are accepted —though their actions might not be. A number of books describe children's negative feelings in a matter-of-fact way, thereby opening the door for further discussion (686, 699, 703, 704, 708).

In their overwhelming desire not to lose their parents' love children often bend over backwards. Winnicott (643) describes the treatment of a little girl who developed destructive feelings of guilt and depression out of fear about her feelings of hatred toward the baby. Moore (664) found children often repress their anger and adopt an attitude of tolerance and nurturance toward the baby—at the expense of creative spontaneity.

Other authors consider the development of tolerance and nurturance, such as caring for the baby, a helpful way for the older child to identify with the parent, rather than compete with the newborn (626, 652). Books for children often emphasize the nurturing role of the older child (676, 681, 684, 685, 699, 706, 707).

Some children who didn't mind babies at all when they were born, bitterly resent toddlers with their cheerful ability to destroy the older child's favorite projects (681). It seems wise to assure the older child some privacy and protection if this seems at all feasible.

Now, what about the younger child's feelings? Do they feel rivalry and jealousy? The second- (or third-, or fourth-) born never had the privilege of being an only child. On the other hand he comes into a family where parents have gained self-confidence in their role as parents. However, later-born children usually run hard and fruitlessly trying to "catch up" with their older sibling. Moreover, older brothers and sisters too often become bossy. These relationships are described graphically in some books for children (677, 678, 683, 695, 697, 698, 705).

Researchers seem to disagree on the effect of birth order on peer relations. Alexander (646) found first-born more popular with peers. Miller and Maruyama (663), on the other hand, found the last-born to be the most popular.

A particularly difficult position seems to be that of being the older siblings of twins (648). Not only does such a child have to share parents, he is also excluded from the special relationship between the twins.

Twins are also discussed in a number of books that try to give help to parents who are suddenly overwhelmed by a houseful of babies (633, 640, 641).

Only children, according to Segal and Yahraes (637), are more dependent and more achieving than first-born. They have a better self-image, more aggression, and less anxiety than other children but consider themselves more powerless in relation to their parents.

Of course, the spacing between children will affect each child. Yahraes (644) found that pacing of siblings more than three years apart improved their sense of competence and the relationship with their parents. Ucko (674) recommends a spacing of four years or more in order to reduce stress in the older child which can create emotional and creative rigidity and reduce intelligence.

In our efforts to examine the feelings and reactions of each individual we often forget to think of the family as a unit, with all kinds of cross-currents and ways of interacting.

Older siblings have been found to influence the cognitive development of the younger (650). Preschoolers facilitate the mastery of the object environment of babies (659). Parents are influenced in the way they perceive their children by the other children in the family (666), and finally, siblings have a strong influence on the personality development of each other (672) and on the way they perceive themselves as boys and girls (669).

After all this turmoil what happens when siblings grow up?

Pafouts (665) describes the strong ambivalent bond between adult siblings. Social comparisons with their brothers and sisters have shaped their identities, their adult roles and peer relations. Adams (645) reports three types of sibling relations among adults: fervent loyalty, rivalry, or solidarity. Bank (647) found intense loyalty among sibling groups of various ages and constellations.

A British film about a family called the relationship of intense, though unwilling bonding *Dear Octopus*. I can think of no better simile.

BIBLIOGRAPHY

Books and Pamphlets for Adults

624. Arnstein, Helen S. *What to Tell Your Child About Birth, Illness, Death, Divorce, and Other Family Crises.* Rev. ed. New York: Condor, 1978.

    Gives sensitive and well thought out advice on how to prepare children for a new baby and how to smooth relationships once the baby arrived.

625. Comer, James P., and Poussaint, Alvin F. *Black Child Care: How to Bring up a Healthy Black Child in America.* New York: Pocket Books, 1975.

    Written in question-and-answer form it gives understanding advice on competitiveness among siblings.

626. Fassler, Joan. *Helping Children Cope: Mastering Stress Through Books and Stories.* New York: The Free Press, 1978.

    Presents the use of children's literature as a help in coping with stressful experiences. The chapter on the new baby contains a sensitive discussion, a review of children's books and general references.

627. Freud, Anna. *Normality and Pathology in Childhood: Assessment of Development.* New York: International Universities Press, 1965.

    Includes a stage-by-stage description "from egocentricity to companionship" which affect a child's ability to relate to a new baby.

628. Ginott, Haim. *Between Parent and Child: New Solutions to Old Problems.* New York: Macmillan, 1965.

Offers many concrete suggestions that will help parents to determine their children's feelings and offers appropriate ways to respond.

629. Hendrick, Joanne. *The Whole Child: New Trends in Early Education.* St. Louis, Mo.: The C. V. Mosby Company, 1980.

Helpful advice for teachers on how to help the child and the child's parents after the arrival of a baby.

630. Isaacs, Susan. *Troubles of Children and Parents.* New York: Schocken Books, 1973. (First published in 1948.)

Contains answers to parents' questions with a full section on "Jealousy" dealing with problems among siblings and problem behavior resulting from sibling rivalry.

631. McDermott, John. *The Complete Book on Sibling Rivalry.* (Formerly titled *Raising Cain and Abel, Too.*) New York: Wideview Books, 1982.

Helpful book that accepts strong feelings and helps parents to deal with them.

632. Murphy, Lois B., and Leeper, Ethel M. *Preparing for Change.* DHEW Publication CD 73-1028. Washington, D.C.: U.S. Department of Health, Education, and Welfare, 1973.

Discusses the teacher's part in helping children to adjust to the arrival of a new baby.

633. Noble, Elizabeth. *Having Twins: A Parents Guide to Pregnancy, Birth, and Early Childhood.* New York: Houghton Mifflin, 1980.

Helpful guide, especially for parents whose twin pregnancy is diagnosed early.

634. Pomerantz, Virginia E., and Schultz, Dodi. *The First Five Years: A Relaxed Approach to Child Care.* Garden City, N.Y.: Doubleday, 1973.

Provides wise and thoroughgoing advice in chapter: "Kissing Kin: Smart Solutions to Sibling Problems."

635. Read, Katherine, and Patterson, June. *The Nursery School and Kindergarten: Human Relationships and Learning.* 7th ed. New York: Holt, Rinehart & Winston, 1980.

Suggests that a new baby at home can create feelings of hostility that are expressed in school.

636. Spock, Benjamin. *Benjamin Spock's Baby and Child Care.* Rev. ed. New York: Pocket Books, Inc., 1965.

This classic contains sound advice for parents on sibling rivalry.

637. Segal, Julius, and Yahraes, Herbert. *A Child's Journey: Forces That Shape the Lives of Our Young.* New York: McGraw-Hill, 1978.

Reports that only children are more dependent and more achieving than firstborn. They have a better self-image, more aggression, and less anxiety than other children, but they consider themselves more powerless vis-a-vis their parents.

638. Stone, L. Joseph, and Church, Joseph. *Childhood and Adolescence.* 4th ed. New York: Random House, 1979.

Discusses the feelings of toddlers at the arrival of a new baby.

639. Sutton-Smith, Brian, and Rosenberg, B. G. *The Sibling.* New York: Holt, Rinehart, & Winston, 1970.

Examines the effects brothers and sisters have upon each other.

640. Theroux, Rosemary T., and Tingley, Josephine F. *The Care of Twin Children: A Commonsense Guide for Parents.* Chicago: The Center for Study of Multiple Gestation, 1978.

Helpful guide that deals with the practical and emotional issues that have to be dealt with in bringing up twins.

641. The Twin Mothers Club of Bergen County, N.J. *And Then There Were Two: A Handbook for Mothers and Fathers of Twins.* Rev. ed. New York: Child Study Association of America, 1971.

Discusses the specific problems parents face when they have twins, including the suddenly increased demands on parents' time and energy.

642. Thomas, Alexander, and Chess, Stella. *Temperament and Development.* New York: Brunner/Mazel, 1977.

Found that response to new babies depends on both temperamental and environmental factors, i.e., birth order, age, degree of prior parental involvement.

643. Winnicott, Donald. *The Piggle.* New York: International Universities Press, 1977.

Presents the psychoanalytic treatment of a little girl who showed serious signs of disturbance after her sister was born, when she was 21 months old. Description of dramatic personality change due to feelings of depression and guilt resulting from the fear of feeling hatred.

644. Yahraes, Herbert. *Developing a Sense of Competence in Young Children.* Rockville, Md.: National Institute of Mental Health, DHEW, 1978. Also available in ERIC Document Reproduction Service, ED 178 191, 1978.

Examines the development of competence in children as affected by interaction with parents, experiences during the "negative stage" (6–24 months) and the pacing of siblings closer than three years apart.

Studies and Articles

645. Adams, Virginia. "The Sibling Bond: A Lifelong Love/Hate Dialectic." *Psychology Today* 15 (June 1981):32–47. Reprinted in *Human Development 82/83*, edited by Hiram E. Fitzgerald and Thomas H. Carr, pp. 228–234. Guilford, Conn.: Dushkin Publishing Group, 1982.

Reports that sibling relations among adults are of three types: fervent loyalty, rivalry, or solidarity.

646. Alexander, C. Norman. "Ordinal Position and Sociometric Status." *Sociometry* 29 (1966):41–51.

Found that first-born are generally more popular with peers.

647. Bank, Stephen. "Hansels and Gretels: A Study of Extremely Loyal Sibling Groups." ERIC Document Reproduction Service, ED 179 312, 1979.

Examined intense sibling loyalty in three sibling groups: (1) four brothers in mid-life, aged 36–45, three of whom were married; (2) two brothers, aged 20 and 22, attending the same university; and (3) a brother aged 6 and his sister age 9 living together in a foster home. Anecdotal excerpts from extensive videotaped interviews are used to illustrate what sibling solidarity is and how it is demonstrated, to show how such strong attachments are formed, and to identify the benefits and burdens of such loyalty.

648. Bernstein, Beth A. "Siblings of Twins." In *The Psychoanalytic Study of the Child*, pp. 135–154. Vol. 35. New Haven: Yale University Press, 1980.

Describes the feelings of older siblings of twins, who in addition to having to share parents, also suffer from being left out of the special relationship between the twins.

649. Bryant, Brenda, and Crockenberg, Susan B. "Correlates and Dimensions of Prosocial Behavior: A Study of Female Siblings with Their Mothers." *Child Development* 51 (1980):529–544.

Investigates the maternal, siblings, and situational correlates of prosocial behavior between siblings and the relationship of prosocial to antisocial behavior.

650. Ciccirelli, Victor G. "Sibling Interaction and Cognitive Development." In *The Developing Individual in a Changing World*, edited by Klaus F. Riegel and John A. Meecham. Vol. 2: *Social and Environmental Issues*, pp. 715–722. The Hague: Mouton, 1976.

Analyzed a number of studies and found that older siblings seem to have an influence on the cognitive development of the younger.

651. Dunn, Judy, and Kendrick, Carol. "The Arrival of a Sibling: Changes of Patterns of Interaction Between Mother and Firstborn Child." *Journal of Child Psychology and Psychiatry and Allied Disciplines* 21 (1980):119–132.

Studied the interaction between mother and first-born child before and after the second child. Found that maternal attention toward the first-born decreased and that there were more confrontations as a result of the changes in the child's behavior.

652. ———. "The Reaction of First-Born Children to the Birth of a Sibling: Mothers' Reports." *Journal of Child Psychology and Psychiatry and Allied Disciplines* 22 (1981):1–18.

Found that when children were interested in the baby there was less clinging, tearfulness, and withdrawal.

653. Elkind, David. "Children's Conception of Brother and Sister." *The Journal of Genetic Psychology*, 1962, pp. 129–136.

Found three stages in the development of the concept "brother": non-differentiated, concretely differentiated, and abstract. The concept of "having a brother" also has three stages: asymmetrical, intuitively symmetrical, and abstractly symmetrical. The ability to comprehend the nature of the relationship will affect the relationship itself.

654. Everson, Sally. "Sibling Counseling." *American Journal of Nursing*, April 1977, pp. 644–646.

Describes behavior problems and feelings of guilt in siblings of a child with a chronic illness.

655. Goldings, Herbert J. "Jump Rope Rhymes and the Rhythm of Latency Development in Girls." In *The Psychoanalytic Study of the Child*, pp. 431–450. Vol. 29. New Haven: Yale University Press, 1974.

Suggests that some games can turn a passive experience into an active one thereby helping to master trauma. Things like a jump rope rhyme:

I had a little brother
His name was Tiny Tim
I put him in the washtub
To teach him how to swim.
He drank up all the water,
Ate up all the soap,
He died last night
With a bubble in his throat.

Helps pre-adolescent girls to come to terms with a younger sibling.

656. Hilton, Irma. "Differences in the Behavior of Mothers Toward First- and Later-Born Children." *Journal of Personality and Social Psychology* 7 (1967):282–290.

First-born chlidren were found to be more dependent than their siblings and their mothers were more interfering, extreme, and inconsistent in their behavior toward them.

657. Jacobs, Blanche, and Moss, Howard A. "Birth Order and Sex of Sibling as Determinants of Mother Infant Interaction." *Child Development* 47 (1976):315–322.

Found that mothers spent less time in social, affectionate, and caretaking interaction with their second child than with the first, especially if the second-born was a girl. This difference seems partly due to the demands of the older child.

658. Kaplan, Elizabeth Bremner. "Manifestation of Aggression and Latency and Preadolescent Girls." In *The Psychoanalytic Study of the Child*, pp. 63–78. Vol. 31. New Haven: Yale University Press, 1976.

Points out that sibling rivalry has its positive side. It can decrease hostile aggression in pre-teen peer relations.

659. Lamb, Michael E. "The Development of Sibling Relationships in Infancy: A Short-Term Longitudinal Study." *Child Development* 49 (1978):1189–1196.

Results suggest that preschool age siblings may facilitate mastery of the object environment by infants.

660. ———. "Interaction Between Eighteen-Month-Olds and Their Preschool Age Siblings." *Child Development* 49 (1978):51–59.

Studied infants and their preschool age siblings at a six month interval.

661. Legg, Cecily; Sherick, Ivan; and Wadland, William. "Reaction of Preschool Children to the Birth of a Sibling." *Child Psychiatry and Human Development* 5 (1974):3–39.

Found that the stress of the birth of a new baby is greatly diminished if the father is able to give the older sibling increased attention. Examines many other factors, such as preparation for the birth of a sibling, the effect of the mother's absence, and of mother-substitutes; sleeping arrangements, imaginary companions, and regressions.

662. Lewis, M., and Gallas, H. "Cognitive Performance in the 12 Week Old Infant: The Effects of Birth Order, Spacing, Sex, and Social Class." In *Research Bulletin*. Princeton, N.J., 1976.

Found the early mother-child relationship is significantly enhanced by wide age differences between children.

663. Miller, Norman, and Maruyama, Geoffrey. "Ordinal Position and Peer Popularity." *Journal of Personality and Social Psychology* 33 (1976):123-131.

Found last-born children most popular with their peers.

664. Moore, Terence. "Stress in Normal Childhood." *Human Relations* 22 (1969):235-250.

Found that children coped with the stress of being displaced by a baby by repressing their anger and adopting an attitude of tolerance and nurturance at the expense of creative spontaneity.

665. Pafouts, Jane H. "Sibling Relationships: A Forgotten Dimension." *Social Work* 21 (1976):200-203.

Describes the strong ambivalent bonds between siblings. Reports on effects that social comparison exerts on brothers, shaping their identity, adult roles, and peer relations.

666. Rosenblatt, Paul, and Skoogberg, Elizabeth L. "Birth Order in Cross-Cultural Perspective." *Developmental Psychology* 10 (1974):48-54.

Found that the way parents perceive each child and the way parents are perceived is influenced by siblings.

667. Rothbart, Maryk. "Sibling Position, Sex and Maternal Involvement. In *The Developing Individual in a Changing World*, edited by Klaus F. Riegel and John A. Meecham, eds. Vol. 2: *Social and Environmental Issues*, pp. 697-706. The Hague: Mouton, 1976.

Report on studies of the role of the mother to her children as affected by birth order.

668. Schooler, Carmi. "Birth Order Effects: Not Here, Not Now!" *Psychological Bulletin* 78 (1972):161-175.

Reports that research reveals no reliable evidence that birth order has a predictable effect on personality or on the treatment of children by their parents.

669. Seegmiller, Bonni R.; Suter, Barbara; and Dunivant, Noel. "Personal, Socioeconomic, and Sibling Influences on

Sex-Role Differentiation." ERIC Document Reproduction Service, ED 176 896, 1978.

Investigated the influences of personal, socioeconomic, and sibling characteristics on the sex-role differentiation of preschool children. Found that sex-role differentiation was most strongly affected by siblings, that siblings had different effects depending upon their own sex, and the sex and/or age of the child concerned. Ordinal position and number of children in the family also influenced sex-role differentiation.

670. Shapiro, Vivian; Fraiberg, Selma; and Adelson, Edna. "Infant-Parent Psychotherapy on Behalf of a Child in a Critical Nutritional State." In *The Psychoanalytic Study of the Child*, pp. 461–491. Vol. 31. New Haven: Yale University Press, 1976.

Describes a teen-age mother who transfers her rivalry toward her younger sister upon her baby.

671. Thomas, Evelyn B.; Turner, Ann M.; Leiderman, Herbert; and Barnett, Clifford B. "Neonate-Mother Interaction: Effects of Parity on Feeding Behavior." *Child Development* 41 (1970):1103–1111.

Results of studying mother-baby interaction indicate that mothers of firstborn children are more demanding, persistent, and conscientious.

672. Toman, Walter. "On the Extent of Sibling Influence." In *The Developing Individual in a Changing World*, edited by Klaus F. Riegel and John A. Meecham. Vol. 2: *Social and Environmental Issues*, pp. 707–714. The Hague: Mouton, 1976.

Examines research on how siblings affect personality development.

673. Tooley, Kay. "Antisocial Behavior and Social Alienation Post Divorce: The Man of the House and His Mother." *American Journal of Orthopsychiatry* 46 (1976):33–42.

Describes how young boys often try to become "the man of the house" after a divorce.

674. Ucko, L. E. "Early Stress Experiences Revealed in 'World Play' Test at Five Years." *Human Development* 10 (1967): 107–127.

Found that children under psychological stress (separation from mother, birth of a new sibling before the fourth year) showed rigidity in creating play worlds and a lowered IQ.

675. Wagner, Mazie Earle; Schubert, Herman J. P.; and Schubert, Daniel S. P. "Sibship-Constellation Effects on Psychological Development, Creativity, and Health." In *Advances in Child Development and Behavior*, edited by Haynes W. Reese and Lewis P. Lipsitt, pp. 57–148. Vol. 14. New York: Academic Press, 1979.

Presents a comprehensive overview of research and clinical evidence on the effects of family constellation on personality traits.

Books for Children

676. Alexander, Martha. *Nobody Asked Me if I Wanted a Baby Sister*. New York: Dial Press, 1971.

A little boy wants to get rid of his baby sister, until he finds that she can only be comforted by him.

677. ————. *I'll Be the Horse if You'll Play with Me*. New York: Dial Press, 1975.

Shows how older brothers set the tone in play.

678. Amoss, Berthe. *Tom in the Middle*. New York: Harper & Row, 1968.

Tom suffers from being the middle brother.

679. Andry, Andrew C., and Kratka, Suzanne C. *Hi, New Baby: A Book to Help Your Child Learn About the New Baby*. New York: Simon & Schuster, 1970.

This factual book shows children what they were like as babies and how they have grown, and what it is like to have a new baby in the family.

680. Arnstein, Helen S. *Billy and Our New Baby*. New York: Behavioral Publications, 1973.

Shows common reactions children have to babies: competition, regression, imitation of infancy. Bill learns to see his own worth and begins to accept the baby.

681. Brenner, Barbara. *Nicky's Sister*. Westminster, Md.: Alfred A. Knopf, 1966.

    Depicts a little boy who, when his sister destroys a favorite toy, decides to run away.

682. Byars, Betsy. *Go and Hush the Baby*. New York: Viking, 1971.

    Shows how family warmth can compensate for delayed gratification.

683. Clifton, Lucille. *My Brother's Fine with Me*. New York: Holt, Rinehart, & Winston, 1975.

    When his five year old brother decides to run away from home, Johnny is glad—at first.

684. Gerson, Mary-Joan. *Omotegi's Baby Brother*. New York: Henry Z. Walek, 1974.

    A little Nigerian boy finds a way to make an important contribution to his brother's naming ceremony.

685. Gill, Joan. *Hush, Jon*. Garden City, N.Y.: Doubleday, 1968.

    Jon finds that the new baby is only a disruption of his life. But when the baby responds to him, he begins to accept her.

686. Greenfield, Eloise. *She Come Bringing Me That Little Baby Girl*. Philadelphia: J. B. Lippincott, 1974.

    Narrates in first person a boy's resentment at having a sister. He comes to realize with his parents' help that the baby needs him.

687. ———. *Good News*. New York: Coward McCann & Geoghegan, 1977. (Formerly *Bubbles*.)

    A boy learns to read and rushes home to read to is mother but only his baby sister has time to listen.

688. Hazan, Barbara Shook. *Why Couldn't I Be an Only Kid Like You*. New York: Atheneum, 1975.

    Two boys, one from a large family, the other an only child, find out that the life of the other is not what they imagined.

689. Hoban, Russel C. *A Baby Sister for Frances*. New York: Harper & Row, 1964.

    One of the popular "Frances" series about a little

person-like badger who shows mild jealousy when baby sister is born.

690. Holland, Viki. *We Are Having a Baby*. New York: Scribner, 1972.

   Factual description of pregnancy, birth, and the arrival of the new baby as seen through the eyes of a child. Deals both with events and feelings.

691. Iwasaki, Chihiro. *A New Baby Is Coming to My House*. New York: McGraw-Hill, 1972.

   A little girl waits for her new baby brother to come home from the hospital.

692. Jarrell, Mary. *The Knee-Baby*. New York: Farrar, Straus & Giroux, 1973.

   Emphasizes reassurance and warmth for the older child.

693. Jordan, June. *New Life: New Room*. New York: Thomas Y. Crowell, 1975.

   Three older siblings and their father make room for the new baby in a tight urban apartment.

694. Keats, Ezra Jack. *Peter's Chair*. New York: Harper & Row, 1967.

   Shows a little boy's resentment when "his" chair is transferred to the new baby. He realizes, however, that the chair is too small for him, and that he is a big brother.

695. Kellog, Steven. *Much Bigger Than Martin*. New York: Dial Press, 1976.

   A little boy would like to be bigger than his bossy older brother.

696. Klein, Norma. *If I Had My Way*. New York: Pantheon Books, 1974.

   A small girl fantasizes how life would be if children ran the world.

697. Pearson, Susan. *Monnie Hates Lydia*. New York: Dial Press, 1975.

   Monnie finds it difficult to be a good sport, when her older sister does not appreciate her contributions.

698. Rudolph, Marguerita. *Today Is Not My Birthday*. New York: McGraw-Hill, 1973.

On his older brother's birthday, Henry decides he wants some of the attention.

699. Schick, Eleanor. *Peggy's New Brother*. New York: Macmillan, 1970.

Peggy resents all the attention the new baby is getting but feels better, when she is successful in assisting with the baby's care.

700. Scott, Ann H. *On Mother's Lap*. New York: McGraw-Hill, 1972.

Michael's jealousy is dispelled by the physical proof that there is room for two on mother's lap.

701. Stein, Sara Bonnett. *That New Baby: An Open Family Book for Parents and Children Together*. New York: Walker, 1974.

Factual book presenting a narrative for adults alongside the one for children; presents acceptance of strong feelings connected with the arrival of a new child and offers advice.

702. Steptoe, John. *Stevie*. New York: Harper & Row, 1969.

While not really a new sibling, Stevie enters Robert's family as a part-time foster child, while his single mother works. While resenting the intrusion, Robert misses Stevie when he moves away.

703. Watson, Joan Werner et al. *Sometimes I'm Jealous*. Racine, Wisc.: Golden Press, 1972.

Shows the resentment of a child when the baby receives too much attention. He is helped to weather the crisis by receiving lots of love. "A Read Together Book for Parents and Children created in cooperation with the Menninger Foundation." Includes a "Note to Parents."

704. Wells, Rosemary. *Noisy Nora*. New York: Dial Press, 1973.

Nora feels neglected when the younger children in her home get most of the attention. Written in rhyme.

705. ———. *Don't Spill It Again James*. New York: Dial Press, 1977.

Three stories about James and his sometimes bossy, sometimes tender older brother.

706. Williams, Barbara. *Jeremy Isn't Hungry*. New York: Dutton, 1978.

A little boy's attempts to amuse and feed his baby almost end in disaster.

707. Winthrop, Elizabeth. *I Think He Likes Me*. New York: Harper & Row, 1980.

Eliza has to find out how to play with her new baby brother.

708. Wolde, Gunilla. *Betsy's Baby Brother*. New York: Random House, 1974.

Betsy sometimes resents the time mother spends with the baby, but mostly she feels that he is cuddly and sweet.

709. ———. *Betsy and the Chicken Pox*. New York: Random House, 1976.

Betsy feels neglected when her baby brother has the chicken pox.

710. Zolotov, Charlotte S. *If It Weren't for You*. New York: Harper & Row, 1966.

Reveals the thoughts of an older brother who imagines that he is an only child.

DISCIPLINE

Why Worry about Discipline?

The answers are manifold. First of all, in dealing with young, inexperienced children, it is natural for protective adults to wish to maintain firm control in order to prevent harm. The problem arises as adults realize that complete control is neither feasible nor desirable. The kind of control that was appropriate with a crawling infant, for instance, becomes useless with an active three year old. Control based on fear and humiliation might either encourage revolt or damage the drive for autonomy and initiative, so important for healthy development. Control, for the purpose of safety, is still needed, but it has to be adjusted to developmental stages as well as to individual needs and situations (728, 741, 743, 754, 783, 796, 798, 802).

The second reason that adults wish to control children has to do with the needs of others who relate to the child. As family members, neighbors in a community, or as classmates at school, little children have to make adjustments to their social environments. To some extent such accommodation has to be imposed upon young children before they can comprehend reasons for it. Here again, however, some demands and expectations may be premature or inappropriate in particular instances. The socializing of young children is an ever-present task of parents and teachers. Success will depend to a great extent on the adult's understanding of age-appropriate expectations as well as their ability to enforce the necessary limits (729, 735, 738, 739, 752,

756, 758, 759, 760, 764, 765, 766, 767, 768, 769, 770, 771, 776, 778, 779, 786, 809, 811, 812).

Developmental Expectations

We need to consider how children learn what to do and what not to do. Young babies will, at first, only respond to their own inner urgings. As they become aware of the world around them, their satisfaction or frustration will depend upon whether or not their wishes are fulfilled. We have learned from Erikson (743, 779) that experiences in these early months provide the foundation for a person's sense of basic trust or mistrust. The development of trust allows for the further development of hope and of an inner drive. As infants proceed to interact with important adults in their life, they learn to give as well as to take. They become aware of the wishes and needs of beloved adults and make efforts to please them. Young children are aware of their smallness, helplessness, and their overwhelming need for love and cuddling. They have an overriding need to please and are willing to make real sacrifices to obtain this happy outcome. Thus children allow society to impose its demands on them and become socialized, even when it requires the modification of basic impulses, such as in toilet training. Now, does this mean that toddlers have developed an inner conscience in regard to toileting? No, it simply means that they have come to understand their parents' wishes and are willing (and able) to cooperate. Such cooperation will become possible again and again as long as the child's environment is appropriate, that is, as long as it does not contain too many "don'ts" and there are a sufficient number of acceptable and interesting things to do. Frustration, boredom, and waiting will prevent children from exhibiting their most mature behavior.

As children grow they continue to investigate the world around them. Their investigations will encompass material things and the workings of the outside world. This will lay the foundation of cognitive development. They also explore the fascinating world of adult values and preferences. What is allowed and what is forbidden? When am I considered "good" and when "bad"? Do all adults agree on "do's" and "don'ts"? Children's strong attachment to and identification with adults creates the need to accept many of these do's and don'ts and incorporate these values into their own thinking. This is how conscience develops (711, 712, 716, 719, 737, 742, 747, 755, 761, 764, 765, 766, 767, 768, 769, 786, 787, 792).

Three year olds, who have no real inner conscience, will forego forbidden activities when they are under observation. They will have no compunction, however, when they do not feel observed and may blithely announce that "Mr. Nobody did it." Nor will they understand adults reproaching them for lying.

By the time children are five they may have the beginnings of inner signals about right and wrong. At the age of seven most children have developed a conscience of sorts. Does this mean that they will never misbehave again? Not at all! But it does mean that they will feel a certain amount of guilt when they do misbehave. And they may realize that this feeling is an uncomfortable consequence of wrong-doing.

These early school years are also the time when children become somewhat less emotionally dependent on the adults in their lives and more attached to children their own age. Such peer groups can often counterbalance adult demands, and pressure members to demonstrate their independence of grown-ups by doing deeds that are known by all to be forbidden (751, 752, 753, 757, 759, 775, 804).

But let us go back to much younger children. Behavior psychologists have shown that praising good behavior (reinforcement) and disregarding bad behavior (extinction) can make children behave in the way that adults would like them to (731, 753, 760, 770, 771, 781, 782, 795, 805, 811). Sounds simple, doesn't it?

But children are more complex than guinea pigs. Their behavior might signify inner stress, immaturity, or inadequate understanding. Conditioning them into pre-set behavior might undermine their just-beginning self-esteem and prevent the development of a sense of competence so important for future learning. Desirable responses in the social domain, such as being polite in an automatic fashion, should not be confused with genuine consideration and understanding of the needs of others.

Lillian Katz (795), in discussing the values and pitfalls of behavior modification, points out that simple reinforcement of desirable behavior or extinction of undesirable behavior may at times be entirely appropriate. This approach is suitable when the child's behavior does not express emotional stress, or when it is not the result of inadequate social learning. We must remember that children lack the vocabulary to communicate their anxieties, fears and confusions. Their behavior might be a cry for help that they are unable to express verbally. Merely responding to the irritating symptom of such distress is similar to treating a cold by wiping a child's nose. Where bad behavior is an indication of inner turmoil, the child needs a therapeutic response based on an acceptance of his or her feelings. The child who behaves inappropriately in a social situation, on the other hand, is entitled to be taught the whys and wherefores that will lead to a more acceptable social response.

Diana Baumrind (736, 738, 765-769), in a longitudinal study, has found that the *way* parents handle the control of children will affect not only the present behavior of children but their entire personality, their sense of competence, responsibility, and independence. Baumrind divided parents into three main types. The *authoritarian* parent "values obedience as a virtue and believes in restricting a child's autonomy." Such restrictiveness induces fears and undue submissiveness, according to Baumrind.

The second type, called *authoritative*, "attempts to direct the child's activities in a rational issue-oriented manner." "The child is directed firmly, consistently, and rationally; . . . parent uses power when necessary, and values obedience . . . as well as independence . . . parent listens to child, but does not base decisions solely on child's desires. This type of control is associated with responsible, assertive, and self-reliant behavior in preschool children."

The third type, the *permissive* parent, "behaves in an affirmative, acceptant and benign manner toward the child's impulses and actions" and aims "to give the child as much freedom as is consistent with the child's physical survival. Freedom to permissive parents means absence of restraint." Permissive parents want their children to be independent but the study revealed that these children were more dependent than those of authoritative parents. The Baumrind studies followed children as they grew up and continue to do so.

The ultimate goal of disciplinary practice is healthy growth and development that allows the fully grown adult to make moral decisions with self-confidence and integrity. It is therefore of paramount importance to think of child rearing and discipline not only in terms of the here and now but in terms of the future of the individual and of society. For many years, perhaps as a response to the moralizing mode of child-rearing at the beginning of the century, American adults shrank from the idea of "moral education." However, Jean Piaget (754, 810), in his investigation of the child's cognitive development, outlined the growth of social and moral concepts. Kohlberg and others (742, 746, 783, 798, 810) in this country continued those studies. Kohlberg developed sequential stages or "levels" of moral thinking. The early childhood years, according to Kohlberg, coincided with the "Pre-Moral" level. At this level, the child's orientation is to punishment and obedience; i.e., his or her understanding of right and wrong is determined by their consequences and by the power of those who enunciate rules and labels. In the second stage of the pre-moral level, the child defines "right" as satisfying one's own needs. At the third level, children exhibit a "good-boy," "good-girl" morality; i.e., they have developed a certain sense of what the world considers "good." The fourth stage (and this is usually beyond the limits of early childhood) is the "law and order orientation" where youngsters feel that authority determines what is right or wrong. The fifth stage is probably the most commonly accepted by our society. In that stage, right is defined by people in terms of the generally accepted rights and standards which have social sanctions. The sixth stage defines right by the decision of individual conscience and self-chosen ethical principles.

While Kohlberg and his associates are keenly aware of the need of moral development and value clarification, they would never suggest aiming too far beyond the present stage of moral development in guiding children's moral growth. Kohlberg recommends exposure of children to the *next higher* stage of reasoning only in discussions that deal with making moral choices (783).

Discipline is the most constant concern of those who deal with children. It involves day-by-day survival, an ongoing teaching process, and the movement into more complex, social situations of constantly changing little individuals. No sooner have parents and teachers developed appropriate methods than children have outgrown them. It means differentiating between the scratch that needs a kiss and the one that needs a band-aid. And then, of course, there is the hurt that needs to be seen by the doctor.

It means balancing the needs of children and of those around them. And finally, it means helping future generations to develop into good and effective human beings.

BIBLIOGRAPHY

Books and Pamphlets for Parents

711. Auerbach, Aline Sophie (Bachman). *The Why and How of Discipline*. Rev. ed. New York: Child Study Association of America, 1964.

    Encourages parents to help children to build inner controls.

712. Bernhardt, Karl Schofield. *Discipline and Child Guidance*. New York: McGraw-Hill, 1964.

    Advocates a middle way between freedom and control that eventually allows children to develop self-discipline and lets parents enjoy parenthood.

713. Caplan, Frank, ed. *The Parenting Advisor*. Garden City, N.Y.: Anchor Press/Doubleday, 1977.

    Provides the views of leading authorities on child rearing in the first three years; included is a chapter on discipline.

714. Cattell, Psyche. *Raising Children with Love and Limits*. Chicago: Nelson Hall, 1972.

    Urges clear limits as a help to avoid confusion for children.

715. Comer, James P., and Poussaint, Alvin F. *Black Child Care: How to Bring up a Healthy Black Child in America*. New York: Simon & Schuster, 1971.

    Gives some understanding advice on discipline to inner-city parents ranging from appropriateness and timing of punishment through temper tantrums to disagreement between parents. General handbook covering all ages.

716. Dinkmeyer, Don, and McKay, Gary. *Raising a Responsible Child: Practical Steps to Successful Family Relationships.* New York: Simon & Schuster, 1973.

Provides methods of encouragement as means to achieve self-esteem and inner discipline.

717. Duvall, Evelyn M. *Evelyn Duvall's Handbook for Parents.* Nashville, Tenn.: Boardman Press, 1974.

Recognizes parents' feelings when faced with discipline problems. Helps parents to live with their "imperfections."

718. Faber, Adele, and Mazlish, Elaine. *Liberated Parents, Liberated Children.* New York: Grosset & Dunlap, 1974.

Describes the experience of a group of parents who, under the guidance of Dr. Haim Ginott (721) found that home does not need to be a battleground and that parents do not need to deny their own feelings.

719. Fraiberg, Selma. *The Magic Years: Understanding and Handling the Problems of Early Childhood.* New York: Charles Scribner's Sons, 1959.

This early childhood classic combines Freudian and Piagetian insights to help parents and teachers to understand the way children feel and think.

720. Gardner, Richard A. *Understanding Children: A Parent's Guide to Child Rearing.* Cresskill, N.J.: Creative Therapeutics, 1979.

Examines child rearing problems by explaining underlying feelings and issues, in a lucid non-technical manner.

721. Ginott, Haim G. *Between Parent and Child: New Solutions to Old Problems.* New York: Macmillan, 1965.

Offers many concrete suggestions that will help parents to determine their children's feelings and offers appropriate ways to respond.

722. Gordon, Thomas. *P.E.T. Parent Effectiveness Training.* New York: Peter H. Wyden, 1970.

723. ———. *P.E.T. in Action.* New York: Wyden Books, 1976.

Both books examine discipline problems in terms of

parent-child power struggle. They advocate mutual agreement and respect.

724. Greenberg, Selma. *Right from the Start: A Guide to Nonsexist Child Rearing.* Boston: Houghton Mifflin, 1978.

Focuses especially on problems arising out of society's unequal attitudes to men and women.

725. Harrison-Ross, Phyllis, and Wyden, Barbara. *The Black Child: A Parent's Guide.* New York: Peter H. Wyden, 1973.

Provides understanding and advice for black parents in a chapter on "Black Dimensions of Discipline."

726. Hymes, James L., Jr. *The Child Under Six.* Englewood Cliffs, N.J.: Prentice-Hall, 1963. (8th printing 1971.)

727. ———. *Discipline.* New York: Bureau of Publications, Teachers College, Columbia University, 1949. (7th printing, 1962.)

Provides warm understanding of the ways children and adults function and sometimes fail to synchronize. Profound knowledge presented with charm and simplicity.

728. Ilg, Frances Lillian; Ames, Louise Bates; and Baker, S. M. *Child Behavior: Specific Advice on Problems of Child Behavior.* Rev. ed. New York: Harper & Row, 1981.

Gives age-by-age techniques on handling disciplinary problems in its chapter on "What to Do About Discipline."

729. Isaacs, Susan. *Troubles of Children and Parents.* New York: Schocken Books, 1973. (First published 1948.)

Contains answers to parents' questions with a full section on "Obedience, Discipline and Punishment," which combines wisdom with common sense.

730. Kohl, Herbert. *Growing with Your Children.* Boston: Little, Brown, 1978.

Gives sympathetic advice to parents, based on understanding of the needs of adults as well as of children.

731. Krumboltz, John D., and Krumboltz, Helen Brandhorst. *Changing Children's Behavior.* Englewood Cliffs, N.J.: Prentice-Hall, 1972.

Explains behavior modification techniques.

732. LeShan, Eda. *How to Survive Parenthood.* New York: Random House, 1965.

Helps parents to see themselves, their children, and everyday problems of living together in a more realistic way.

733. Neill, Alexander Sutherland. *Freedom, Not License!* New York: Hart, 1966.

The author of *Summerhill* answers parents' letters on discipline and other problems. Based on the belief that children are basically good and need more freedom.

734. Pomerantz, Virginia E., and Schultz, Dodi. *The First Five Years: A Relaxed Approach to Child Care.* Garden City, N.Y.: Doubleday, 1973.

Gives wise counsel from a pediatrician about everyday problems including discipline.

735. Spock, Benjamin. *Raising Children in a Difficult Time.* New York: Norton, 1974.

Commonsense discussion that should convince detractors that Dr. Spock is not at all "permissive." Helpful chapters on discipline and on "Children Who Could Benefit from Psychotherapy."

736. Yahraes, Herbert. *Parents as Leaders: The Role of Control and Discipline.* U.S. Government Printing Office no. 017-024-00702-1. Washington, D.C.: Superintendent of Documents, 1978. Also available in ERIC Document Reproduction Service, ED 157 622, 1978.

Reviews Diana Baumrind's studies (765–769) on the effects of various kinds of parental discipline.

Books and Pamphlets for Teachers

737. Association for Childhood Education International. *Toward Self-Discipline: A Guide for Parents and Teachers.* 1981.

Contains suggestions for parents, teachers and others about discipline problems and how to help children to develop self-discipline.

738. Baumrind, Diana. *Early Socialization and the Discipline Controversy.* Morristown, N.J.: General Learning Press, 1975.

Presents report on the longitudinal study that found that children are more self-reliant and competent when handled with firm consistency coupled with respect than children of permissive or authoritarian parents.

739. Beyer, Evelyn. *Teaching Young Children*. Indianapolis, Ind.: The Bobbs-Merrill Company, 1968.

Contains a useful discussion on discipline that is not authoritarian or overpermissive.

740. Cohen, Dorothy H., and Rudolph, Marguerita. *Kindergarten and Early Schooling*. Englewood Cliffs, N.J.: Prentice-Hall, 1977.

Chapter "The Meaning of Discipline" provides sound and down-to-earth advice to the teacher of young children.

741. Damon, William. *The Social World of the Child*. San Francisco: Jossey-Bass, 1977.

Describes studies with 4–12 year olds that examine implications of Kohlberg's stages of moral development.

742. Danoff, Judy; Breitbart, Vicky; and Barr, Elinor. *Open for Children*. New York: McGraw-Hill, 1977.

Includes a chapter on "Discipline and Self-Control" that is full of practical advice based on a child-development point of view.

743. Erikson, Erik Homburger. *Childhood and Society*. Rev. ed. New York: Norton, 1964.

Outlines developmental stages that lead to self-control.

744. Ginott, Haim. *Teacher and Child: A Book for Parents and Teachers*. New York: Macmillan, 1972.

Offers many concrete suggestions that will not only help to resolve problems but can change the tenor of teacher-child relationships.

745. Gordon, Thomas. *T.E.T. Teacher Effectiveness Training*. New York: Peter H. Weyden, 1974.

Examines classroom discipline problems in terms of teacher-child power struggle.

746. Henderson, Ronald W., and Bergan, John R. *The Cultural Context of Childhood*. Columbus, Ohio: Charles E. Merrill Publishing Company, 1976.

Provides a good overview of theories of moral development and the development of conscience.

747. Hendrick, Joanne. *The Whole Child: New Trends in Early Education.* 2d ed. St. Louis: C. V. Mosby, 1980.

Contains helpful chapters on helping children to establish self-discipline and on dealing with aggression.

748. Howard, Norma K. *Discipline and Behavior: An Abstract Bibliography.* Urbana, Ill.: Publications Office, ERIC, College of Education, University of Illinois, 1974.

This selective bibliography contains references to 202 ERIC documents on the subjects of discipline and behavior modification of young children. The citations are divided into five sections: (1) regular classroom; (2) teacher training and teaching techniques; (3) exceptional child; (4) family; and (5) general.

749. Hymes, James L., Jr. *Teaching the Child Under Six.* 3rd ed. Columbus, Ohio: Charles E. Merrill, 1981.

Integrates disciplinary concerns into total curricular considerations based on a child development point of view.

750. Kohl, Herbert. *On Teaching.* New York: Schocken Books, 1976.

Written for the elementary school teacher, it contains such universally helpful chapters as "dealing with feelings —one's own and the students'," "Losing Control," etc.

751. Kounin, Jacob S. *Discipline and Group Management in Classrooms.* New York: Holt, Rinehart, & Winston, 1970.

Presents ways to utilize field theory in the classroom by examining the ways teachers, individual students, and classroom groups interact.

752. Murphy, Lois Barkley, and Leeper, Ethel M. *Away from Bedlam.* DHEW Publication OCD 73-1029. Washington, D.C.: Superintendent of Documents, U.S. Government Printing Office, 1973.

Discusses in plain terms how to maintain reasonable order and control in a preschool classroom.

753. Osborne, D. Keith, and Dyson, Janie. *Discipline and Classroom Management.* Athens, Ga.: Education Associates, 1981.

Presents practical suggestions for classroom teachers based on four theoretical modes: psychodynamics, behavior modification, social learning, and field theory.

754. Piaget, Jean. *The Moral Judgment of the CHild*. New York: Free Press, 1965. (First published in French, 1932.)

Hallmark study of moral attitudes that forms the foundation for much of the later work in this area.

755. Read, Katherine, and Patterson, June. *The Nursery School and Kindergarten: Human Relationships and Learning*. 7th ed. New York: Holt, Rinehart, & Winston, 1980.

Presents chapters on "Initial Support Through Guides to Speech and Action"; "Using Discipline"; "Feelings of Hostility and Aggressiveness"; and "Authority and Setting Limits." The chapters as well as the humanistic orientation of the entire book can be helpful to teachers.

756. Redl, Fritz. *When We Deal with Children*. New York: Free Press, 1966.

Contains many suggestions for teachers based on classroom and clinical experience. Special chapter on discipline in classroom practice.

757. ———, and Wattenberg, William W. *Mental Hygiene in Teaching*. New York: Harcourt Brace & World, 1959.

Provides a lucid handbook for teachers who are not only faced with individuals but have to deal with groups. Ego-Psychology and Group Dynamics orientation.

758. Roedell, Wendy Conklin; Slaby, R. G., and Robinson, H. B. *Social Development in Young Children: A Report for Teachers*. Washington, D.C.: U.S. Department of Health, Education, and Welfare, National Institute of Education, 1976.

The chapter "Moral Judgment and Good Behavior" contains many valuable behavior management suggestions.

759. Stone, Jeannette Galambos. *A Guide to Discipline*. Rev. ed. Washington, D.C.: National Association for the Education of Young Children, 1978.

Contains practical advice about how to handle such

discipline situations as spitting, biting, and kicking. It gives many examples of things to say and do that will relieve, control, or prevent tense situations in preschools.

760. Wittes, G., and Radin, N. *Ypsilanti Home and School Handbooks: Helping Your Child to Learn: The Reinforcement Approach.* San Rafael, Calif.: Dimensions Publishing Company, 1969.

Explains reinforcement theory and outlines how to apply it to modify the behavior of young children.

761. Yahraes, Herbert. *Developing a Sense of Competence in Young Children.* Rockville, Md.: National Institute of Mental Health, DHEW, 1978. Also available ERIC Document Reproduction Service ED 178 191, 1978.

Examined the development of competence in children as affected by interaction with parents, experiences during the "negativistic stage" (6–24 months), and the spacing of siblings closer than three years apart.

Studies and Articles

762. Anderson, Luleen S. "The Aggressive Child." *Children Today* 7 (January/February 1978):11.

A useful discussion with many helpful suggestions for parents and teachers on the handling of aggression.

763. Anderson, Rosalie. "Corporal Punishment in the Care of Children: A Literature Review and Analysis." ERIC Document Reproduction Service ED 188 372, 1979.

Presents a broad-based highly readable review of corporal punishment including the summary of dozens of studies and some position papers.

764. Anselmo, Sandra. "Discipline in Day Care Centers." *Child Care Quarterly* 5 (1976):192–197.

Proposes a comprehensive approach to handling discipline in day care centers, discouraging just reacting to a child's misbehavior in favor of establishing an atmosphere and environment in which a child is encouraged to behave in a positive and constructive manner.

765. Baumrind, Diana. "Effects of Authoritative Parental Control on Child Behavior." *Child Development* 37 (1966): 887–907.

766. ———. "Child Care Practice Anteceding Three Patterns of Preschool Behavior." *Genetic Psychology Monographs*, No. 75, 1967.

767. ———. "Current Patterns of Parental Authority." *Developmental Psychology Monographs*, No. 1, 1971.

768. ———. "The Development of Instrumental Competence Through Socialization." In *Minnesota Symposia on Child Psychology*, edited by A. Pick. Vol. 7, pp. 1–46. Minneapolis: University of Minnesota Press, 1973.

769. ———. "Contribution of the Family to the Development of Competence in Children." *Schizophrenia Bulletin* 14 (1975):12–37.

Found that firm, consistent parents who gave reasons and respected the child had self-reliant, competent children. Authoritarian parents, who set absolute rules, used punishment and were not very affectionate, had insecure, hostile children. Permissive parents, who were accepting but ineffective and disorganized, had dependent, immature children with poor self-reliance and poor self-control.

770. Becker, Wesley C. "Reducing Behavior Problems: An Operant Conditioning Guide for Teachers." ERIC Document Reproduction Service ED 034 570, 1969.

Describes step-by-step procedures for reinforcement and extinction followed by increased reward and punishment if the first steps fail.

771. ———. "Consequences of Different Kinds of Parental Discipline." In *Child Development Research*, edited by Martin L. Hoffman and Lois Wladis Hoffman, pp. 169–208. Vol. 1. New York: Russell Sage Foundation, 1964.

Examines the literature on discipline by means of factor analysis as it relates to warmth versus hostility and restrictiveness versus permissiveness.

772. Berkowitz, Leonard. "Control of Aggression." In *Review of Child Development Research*, edited by Bettye M. Caldwell and Henry N. Ricciuti, pp. 95–140. Vol. 3. Chicago: Chicago University Press, 1973.

Concluded after reviewing the research that release of
hostility increases rather than reduces tension.
773. Caldwell, Bettye M. "Aggression and Hostility in Young
Children." *Young Children* 32 (1977):4–13.

Suggests that parents and teachers must help children
to de-escalate their aggressiveness back down to the level
of play.
774. Dodson, Fitzhugh. "How to Discipline with Love." *American
Baby,* January 1979. Reprinted in *Early Childhood Education 80/81,* edited by Judy Spitler McKee, pp. 192–193.
Guilford, Conn.: Dushkin Publishing Group, 1980.

Discusses discipline problems with infants and toddlers
and suggests that parents accept their own feelings and
that they try to "childproof" the environment.
775. Doyle, Walter. "Helping Beginning Teachers Manage
Classrooms." *National Association of Secondary School Principals Bulletin* 59 (1975):38–41.

Presents a framework that emphasizes preventive skills
and group management. Although written for high school
teachers, the principles apply to the early childhood classroom as well.
776. Elardo, Richard. "Values and Childrearing in the Home
and Day Care Center: Issues for the 1980's." ERIC
Document Reproduction Service ED 201 377, 1980.

Discusses the day care center's increasing role in socializing children.
777. ———, and Caldwell, Bettye M. "Value Imposition in Early
Childhood: Fact or Fancy?" *Child Care Quarterly* 2 (1973):
6–13.

Found that day care parents felt children should be
aggressive and defend their rights while teachers discour-
aged aggression.
778. Emmerich, Walter. "The Parental Role: Functional-Cognitive
Approach." *Monographs of the Society for Research in Child
Development* 34, Serial No. 132 (1969).

This study investigated parental roles as related to
parental attitudes. The study pointed to a crisis in parent-

child relations during preschool years due to the child's transition to greater independence at this age. Positive reinforcement (praise) was found effective, while negative reinforcement (scolding, punishment, etc.) was seen as relatively ineffective in reducing unwanted behavior.

779. Erikson, Erik Homburger. "A Healthy Personality for Every Child." In *As The Twig Is Bent: Readings in Early Childhood Education,* edited by Robert Henry Anderson and Harold G. Shane, pp. 120-137. Boston: Houghton Mifflin, 1971.

Adapts Freud's ideas to consider development of the self within the context of society. His eight stages of man's emotional development have influenced our thinking enormously, and help in viewing discipline problems in context of developmental stages.

780. Flynn, T. M. "Parental Attitudes and the Pre-School Child's Self-Concept." ERIC Document Reproduction Service, ED 171 405, 1979.

Found that mothers who advocated more control tended to have sons with higher self-concepts, that both mothers and fathers of girls advocated significantly more control than mothers and fathers of boys.

781. Forehand, Rex; Roberts, Mark W.; Doleys, Daniel M.; Hobbs, Steven A.; and Resick, Patricia A. "An Examination of Disciplinary Procedures with Children." *Journal of Experimental Psychology* 21 (1976):109-120.

Describes experiments that found that negative attention (extinction) decreased noncompliance more effectively than negative commands.

782. Franklin, Marjorie B., and Biber, Barbara. "Psychological Perspectives and Early Childhood Education: Some Relations Between Theory and Practice." In *Current Topics in Early Childhood Education,* edited by Lillian G. Katz. Vol. 1. Norwood, N.J.: Ablex Publishing Corp., 1977.

Contrasts the behavioristic point of view with the cognitive-developmental and the developmental-interactive approaches.

783. George, Paul S. "Discipline, Moral Development, and Levels of Schooling." *Educational Forum* 45 (1980):57-67.

Relates each of Kohlberg's six stages of moral development to the appropriate level of schooling and method of classroom discipline. Concludes that teachers can successfully solve discipline problems by choosing strategies from a stage just beyond the student's level.

784. Gray, Dianne Elaine. "The Teacher's Role in Understanding Aggression and Dealing with It Effectively in the Preschool Environment." ERIC Document Reproduction Service, ED 200 334, 1981.

Explores the role of the preschool teacher in dealing effectively with aggression in the classroom setting. Preventive and interventive approaches to dealing with aggression are suggested, including the control of space and room arrangement, the control of time, and the reinforcement of altruistic and appropriate behaviors. Intervention approaches advocated include emotional release through physical activities, the controlled use of sound to direct emotional states, and dramatic play. Steps for leading nonplaying aggressive children toward participation in social play are described.

785. Harrington, David M.; Block, Jeanne H.; and Block, Jack. "Intolerance of Ambiguity in Preschool Children: Psychometric Considerations, Behavioral Manifestations and Parental Correlates." *Developmental Psychology* 14 (1978):242–256.

Authoritarian fathers were found to have anxious children who could not tolerate ambiguity and were restricted in their cognitive functioning.

786. Harwell, Helen B., and Harwell, John E. "An Exploratory Study of Social Values in Kindergartens." *Journal of the International Association of Pupil Personnel Workers* 25 (1981): 116–123.

Half the kindergarten children studied lacked leadership ability and appeared to be followers. Many lacked initiative, intellectual curiosity, and the ability to take constructive criticism. The authors suggest that schools have a responsibility to provide an environment free from deprivation of social values and urge that internal self-discipline replace external discipline.

787. Hatano, Giyoo; Miyake, Kazuo; and Tajima, Nabumoto. "Mother Behavior in Unstructured Situations and Child's Acquisition of Number Conservation." *Child Development* 51 (1980):379–385.

Found that excessive directiveness by mothers reduced children's spontaneous exploration and slowed cognitive development.

788. Hendrick, Joanne. "Aggression: What to Do About It!" *Young Children* 23 (1968):298–305.

Suggests a number of acceptable substitute activities that can release bottled up feeling. Urges sublimation.

789. Hesch, Patricia Yunker. "Children Live by Rules/Let Them Help Make Them." *Day Care and Early Education* 7 (1979): 12–15.

Suggests some ways that teachers can establish and maintain appropriate behavior in preschool children in day care centers.

790. Hipple, Marjorie L. "Classroom Discipline Problems: Fifteen Humane Solutions." *Childhood Education* 54 (1978): 183–187.

Cites situations every teacher will recognize and provides comfortable solutions.

791. Hoffman, Martin L. "Parent Discipline and the Child's Consideration for Others." *Chlid Development* 34 (1963): 573–588.

792. ———. "Personality and Social Development." *Annual Review of Psychology* 28 (1977):295–321.

Found that parents who are less assertive will have children who are more considerate for other people's needs, while strongly assertive discipline appears to cause social withdrawal and impulse control based on fear.

793. Huffine, Susan; Silvern, Steven B.; and Brooks, Douglas M. "Teacher Responses to Contextually Specific Sex Type Behaviors in Kindergarten Children." *Education Research Quarterly* 4 (1979):29–35.

Kindergarten teachers were more likely to discipline when boys were verbally disruptive, but disciplined girls for disruptive aggressive behaviors. Teachers were physical when responding to boys' disruptions and used verbal and nonverbal behaviors when responding to girls' disruptive behaviors. Girls' questions received longer teacher responses.

794. Hyman, Irwin A., and Lally, Dolores. "Discipline in the 1980's: Some Alternatives to Corporal Punishment." *Children Today* 11 (1982):10-13.

Describes the work of the National Center for the Study of Corporal Punishment and Alternatives in the Schools at Temple University, Philadelphia, Pennsylvania. The center offers workshops, advocacy, research, and information programs in order to help teachers to generate a rich repertoire of theoretical and practical solutions to discipline problems.

795. Katz, Lillian. "Condition with Caution." *Young Children* 27 (1972): 27-280.

Urges examination of causes of behavior and of underlying feelings before applying the tools of behavior modification. Suggests that other forms of treatment, such as teaching or therapy, are indicated in many instances.

796. Kohlberg, Lawrence. "The Development of Children's Orientations Towards a Moral Order: Sequence in the Development of Moral Thought." In *The Process of Child Development*, edited by Peter B. Neubauer. New York: Jason Aronson, Inc., 1976.

A lucid explanation of Kohlberg's six stage theory of moral development, well written and giving good examples of the attitudes characterizing each stage. A more complete description of the six stages can be found in the *Journal of Philosophy*, October 1973, pp. 164-165.

797. McDaniel, Thomas R. "Identifying Discipline Problems: A Self-Evaluation Exercise." *Childhood Education* 57 (1981): 223-226.

Helps teachers to evaluate children's behavior in terms of the effect it has on their learning and social growth.

798. Martorella, Peter H. "Selected Early Childhood Affective

Learning Programs: An Analysis of Theories, Structure, and Consistency." *Young Children* 30 (1975):289-301.

Reviews four commercially available affective programs, including one based on Kohlberg's work. Three of the four begin at the four-year-old level; all appear to be based exclusively on group discussion of values and situations.

799. Mondell, Sid, and Tyler, Forrest B. "Parental Competence and Styles of Problem-Solving Play Behavior with Children." *Developmental Psychology* 17 (1981):73-78.

Children were found to be more competent in unexpected situations if their parents were warm, offered praise, and occasional modeling.

800. Mulhern, Raymond K., and Passman, Richard H. "Children's Gender and Responsiveness to Their Parents: Influence on Parental Discipline." Paper presented at the Annual Convention of APA, 1979. ERIC Document Reproduction Service, ED 178 223, 1979.

Reports on a reinforcement experiment that showed correlations between children's gender and responsiveness to reward or punishment with parents being more punitive toward children of the opposite sex.

801. Ostfeld, Barbara. "We've Been Asked." *Day Care and Early Childhood Education*, November 1974. Reprinted in *Readings in Early Childhood Education 77/78*, edited by Judy Spitler McKee, pp. 218-219. Guilford, Conn.: Dushkin Publishing Group, 1977.

Offers specific suggestions for coping with disruptive behavior in preschool environments. Emphasis on a "yes" environment and on physical safety.

802. Parke, Ross D. "Rules, Roles and Resistance to Deviation: Recent Adances in Punishment, Discipline and Self-Control." In *Minnesota Symposia of Child Psychology*, edited by A. D. Pick, pp. 111-143. Vol. 8. University of Minnesota Press, 1975.

803. ———. "Some Effects of Punishment on Children's Behavior—Revisited." In *Contemporary Readings in Child Psychology*, edited by Mavis E. Hetherington and Ross D. Parke, pp. 208-220. New York: McGraw-Hill, 1977.

Found on reviewing research that corporal punishment is only effective when administered by nurturant parents. He suggests that it is not the physical punishment but the parental disapproval that children respond to.

804. Redl, Fritz, and Sheviakov, George V. "Discipline in Classroom Practice." In *When We Deal with Children*, edited by Fritz Redl, pp. 254-308. New York: The Free Press, 1966.

Discusses group factors that affect classroom discipline.

805. Risley, Todd R., and Baer, Donald H. "Operant Behavior Modification: The Deliberate Development of Behavior." In *Child Development and Social Policy: Review of Child Development and Research*, edited by Bettye M. Caldwell and Henry N. Ricciuti, pp. 283-329. Vol. 3. Chicago: University of Chicago Press, 1973.

Comprehensive review of the theory of operant conditioning and research on the subject.

806. Rocke, Edward J. "Parent Variables in Young Children's Cooperative Behavior." ERIC Document Reproduction Service, ED 183 722, 1980.

Found that while mothers' discipline was unrelated to cooperation, fathers' discipline tended to be positively related to daughters' cooperativeness and negatively related to sons'. Fathers' affection tended to be related to sons' cooperativeness and mothers' affection to daughters' cooperativeness.

807. Sherman, James A., and Bushell, Don, Jr. "Behavior Modification as an Education Technique. In *Review of Child Development Research*, edited by Frances Degen Horowitz, E. Mavis Hetherington, Sandra K. Scarr-Salapate, and Gerald M. Siegel, pp. 409-462. Vol. 4. Chicago: University of Chicago Press, 1975.

Presents studies related to the classroom application of behavior modification techniques.

808. Siegel, Alberta Engvall, and Kohn, Lynette Gayle. "Permissiveness, Permission, and Aggression: The Effects of Adult Presence or Absence on Aggression in Children." In *Child Development and Behavior*, edited by Freda Rabelsky and Lynn Dorman, pp. 234-242. New York: Alfred A. Knopf, 1970.

Found that adult non-interference in aggressive behavior is interpreted by children as permission.

809. Staub, Ervin. "Socialization by Parents and Peers and Experiential Learning of Prosocial Behavior." In *Mother/ Child, Father/Child Relationships*, edited by Joseph H. I. Stevens and Marylin Mathews, pp. 69–84. Washington, D.C.: National Association for the Education of Young Children, 1978.

Discusses parents' disciplinary practices in relation to developing socially desirable behavior.

810. Turiel, Elliot. "Stage Transition in Moral Development." In *Second Handbook of Research on Teaching*, edited by Robert Morris and William Travers, pp. 732–758. Chicago: Rand McNally & Company, 1973.

Provides clear, comprehensive review of research and theory based on Piaget's and Kohlberg's levels of moral development.

811. Walters, Richard H.; Parke, Ross D.; and Cane, Valerie A. "Timing of Punishment and the Observation of Consequences to Others as Determinants of Response Inhibition." *Journal of Experimental Child Psychology* 2 (1965): 10–30.

Found that rebuke or punishment is more effective when administered at the beginning of aggressive behavior.

812. Weller, Leonard, and Kerkowitz, E. "Parental Discipline and Delayed Gratification." *Social Behavior and Personality* 3 (1975):229–232.

Found that children brought up by less coercive parents are better able to delay gratification than those raised under coercive power.

SOCIAL RELATIONSHIPS

Parents sending their child to any kind of play group or preschool will consider the companionship of other children one of the prime benefits for their own child. Usually they find, however, that far from joining immediately in mutually satisfying play, children, at first, don't even seem to notice each other. Social interaction has to be learned.

How does such knowledge develop? How does the human infant, who at first does not even know where he ends and his mother begins (822, 859), learn "how to make friends and influence people"?

The "hatching" of the human infant was described in detail in the section on *Separation*. Kohlberg (871) describes how the mother, once recognized as a separate person, becomes the infant's first playmate. However, it was found (859) that in the first interactions with other persons the baby will think of these persons as objects that need to be inspected and manipulated in the same way that he thinks of his rattle or his own hands and feet. Even if children less than one year old are in a day-care program, their attention will center on toys and other objects rather than people, according to Muller and Lucas (882). During the beginning of the second year children begin to demonstrate their interest in other toddlers and engage in "simple and complex interchanges."

The child at this age is totally egocentric as described by Piaget (826). This means that he is unable to see things from a perspective other than his own and disregards the effect of his actions upon others. Selman and Byrne (890) found that even at four years of age 80 percent of all children were convinced that other children had the same thoughts and beliefs they had—they were still egocentric.

The toddler joyfully interacts with other children—but does not consider them as people just as real as he is, even though he does on occasion identify with others and respond sympathetically to their distress (869). Conflicts are usually resolved physically by grabbing or hitting (835).

Mueller and Lucas (882) found that near two years, toddlers begin to have "complementary interchanges" where they are able to formalize some games to the extent that they know what to expect from the other child. Robert W. White (905) considers the toddler age, with its growth of mobility, the basis for the growth of self-esteem.

As the child turns three he detects, according to White, the consequence of locomotion, linguistic understanding, and imagination. He also develops a growing ability to comprehend and to try out various social rules. These actions can lead to a further development of a sense of competence, to the first loosening of egocentrism, and to the beginnings of the understanding of others.

We must remember that young children have difficulty following a train of thought "in their head." They must think through action. This is why play is all important in the development of children's understanding. Children think through play. The child who is not able to "de-center," i.e., to take the perspective of another person in thought, might be able to do so in socio-dramatic play. Children will spontaneously explore what it "feels like" to be a mother, a teacher, a baby, a doctor, or whatever else puzzles them by acting out these roles. They (literally, often) step into the shoes of another. Role playing as the instrument of social learning has been described by many (838, 845, 848, 853, 863, 868, 881, 906). Cuffaro (855) depicts the way children learn to distance from themselves and to define themselves in relation to the world, social and physical, through building with blocks and looking at the world from the outside, as it were.

Hirsch (868) discusses the ways children become less egocentric by (1) taking the role of others through dramatic play; (2) their interacting with other children in a preschool classroom facilitates and supports positive interaction (see also 833, 865, 867); (3) they become acquainted with their community through field trips; and (4) they symbolize their growing understanding of the social world through block-building and other representational activities; (5) children learn to empathize with others through listening to stories (see also 814, 845 and the list of books for children 910–935); and finally (6) children learn to accept individual differences and the fact that others have feelings different from their own through teacher modeling.

Modeling is the major emphasis of Bandura's work (813) and is discussed by Marcus and Leiserson (879). Prosocial behavior can also develop through peer modeling (887, 901).

Interaction with other preschoolers on a day-by-day basis provides the opportunity for the development of social skills through trial and error (816). That peer interaction facilitates and expedites social development has been demonstrated and described by a number of authors (820, 854, 864, 899). As social awareness grows, egocentricity diminishes (819, 862). Butler (852) describes how growing and learning in a good preschool environment develops children's sense of self and makes them valuable group members.

Teachers wishing to help children to develop to their fullest potential emotionally, intellectually as well as socially must be aware of the effects and dynamics of group interaction. Rubin (888) describes the way the peer group can help children to develop a sense of group belonging and self-understanding. Kounin (821) and Redl (828, 829) show how classroom discipline depends on the teacher's understanding of group factors. The climate of the classroom is influenced by the teacher (833). Hallinan (865) found that open classrooms did not have "stars" and "social isolates" the way traditional classes did. Harwell and Harwell (867) describe many kindergartens as bereft of social values and demonstrate that initiative, intellectual curiosity, personal ego-strength, and leadership ability cannot flourish in a rigid environment with emphasis on external discipline.

In well-functioning groups peer leaders will emerge. Such leaders are usually helpful to their peers in solving interpersonal conflicts through asking and helping (870). In some groups leadership roles depend on perceived toughness (898). The ability of preschoolers to develop their own structure, design their own rules and solve their own problems was demonstrated by Turner (837). Group interaction can produce problems of its own, as described by Sherman (897) and Redl (828).

Studies found (850) that preschoolers are more cooperative and less competitive than older children, even though older children tend to be more helpful. Orlick (825) differentiates between cooperative and competitive types of competition.

Social interaction in mixed age groups was compared with same-age groups by Hartup (866) who found that both constellations are valuable although their influence on development differs. Bizman found (846) that children in mixed age groups were more altruistic than those in homogeneous age groups. Furman et al. (860) suggest that shyness and social isolation can be overcome more easily if a child has opportunities to play with younger children.

Aggression behavior is rated by most teachers as the major problem in group interaction. Gray (863) finds that a great deal of aggression can be prevented by eliminating frustration caused by crowding, poor arrangement of space, poor use of time, excessive noise, and inappropriate activities. Shantz and Schomer (895) observed preschoolers and noted that most aggression was caused by territorial disputes rather than fights over possessions. Teachers will respond with mixed feelings to a study by Raph et al. (884) who found that children became less aggressive with each other the longer they attended preschool; however, aggression toward teachers increased with length of attendance. (Further discussion on aggression will be found in the section on *Strong Feelings*.)

Boys are usually more aggressive than girls. Maccoby and Jacklin (876) find this prevalent in many cultures and conclude that this difference has a biological basis. Tieger (904) disagrees and states that this contention has neither an empirical nor a theoretical foundation. Eron (857) proposes that boys be subjected to the same training that girls receive traditionally in order to encourage sensitivity and nurturant, socially positive behavior. When it comes to resolution of conflicts Selman (835) found that children under seven are still egocentric. They believe that the conflict was *caused* by one party and is *felt* by the other. Selman calls this an "unrelated solution." Teachers can clarify for children the feelings of the other person and thereby facilitate de-centering.

As children continue to distance themselves from their parents the importance of the peer group and of individual friendships becomes more important in their lives. By the time they enter elementary school they begin to be able to appreciate others as separate and distinct personalities (818, 835, 859, 869, 882), and they begin to be able to take the perspective of the other person (819, 826, 843, 890).

Selman (891) concluded a systematic study of the development of the concept of friendship as children mature. He found that social relationships develop in consequential stages, each of which requires a reorganization of mental schemata along lines described by Piaget. The preoperational child (3–7 years) reflects on the physical attributes of and the shared activities with playmates he calls friends. "He is my friend because he is nice." In the primary grades (6–8 years) the child thinks of friendship as "one-way assistance." "A friend does things that please me." Only by 9 to 12 years does the child really become aware of the reciprocal nature of friendship.

Friendship in the early childhood years is a far cry from adult friendship as described by Rubin (888) as a "nonfamilial relationship likely to foster a feeling of belonging and a sense of identity." But lest we become impatient with the young child's incomplete attainments, let us consider the long way he has traveled in these few years. He started out not even sure of himself as a separate person. Now he is well on his way to become a separate entity in the social world.

BIBLIOGRAPHY

Books and Pamphlets for Adults

813. Bandura, Albert. *Social Learning Theory*. Englewood Cliffs, N.J.: Prentice-Hall, 1977.

    Discusses the acquisition of social skills and the role of modeling.

814. Brearly, Molly, ed. *The Teaching of Young Children: Some Applications of Piaget's Learning Theory*. New York: Schocken Books, 1970.

    Discusses ways egocentricity diminishes as children develop the ability to "think" themselves into the position of another person through listening to stories and through social experiences.

815. Cohen, Dorothy. *The Learning Child: Guidelines for Parents and Teachers*. New York: Vintage Books, 1973.

    Describes "tattling" as the function of a newly acquired conscience that needs to let the adult know that the "tattler" knows right from wrong.

816. ———, and Rudolph, Marguerita. *Kindergarten and Early Schooling*. Englewood Cliffs, N.J.: Prentice-Hall, 1977.

    Describes the trial and error learning that results in social skills in kindergarten.

817. Coles, Robert. *Children of Crisis*. Vols. 1–5. New York: The Atlantic Monthly Press, various dates.

    Contains sensitive descriptions of the impact of discrimination on black children and on growing up in various subcultures, i.e., migrants, northern children, Eskimos, Chicanos, Indians, and the wealthy.

818. Damon, William. *The Social World of the Child.* San Francisco: Jossey-Bass Publishers, 1977.

Describes progressive developmental changes in social relationships and social judgment of children 4–12.

819. Flavell, John H.; Botkin, Patricia T.; Fry, Charles L., Jr.; Wright, John W.; and Jarvis, Paul E. *The Development of Role Taking and Communication Skills in Children.* New York: John Wiley & Sons, 1968.

Found that late preschool children have learned to infer the perspective of others, i.e., that they are capable of developing early role taking schemes.

820. Hymes, James L., Jr. *The Child Under Six.* 8th ed. Englewood Cliffs, N.J.: Prentice-Hall, 1971.

Provides understanding of the ways children live in groups and grow in their social skills.

821. Kounin, Jacob S. *Discipline and Group Management in Classrooms.* New York: Holt, Rinehart, & Winston, 1970.

Shows how classroom discipline is dependent on the teacher's understanding of group processes.

822. Mahler, Margaret S.; Pine, Fred; and Bergman, Anni, *The Psychological Birth of the Human Infant: Symbiosis and Individuation.* New York: Basic Books, 1975.

Describes the gradual emergence of a "sense of self" as children around the age of 1½ to 2 gradually are able to view themselves as entities separate from their mothers.

823. Margolin, Edythe. *Sociocultural Elements in Early Childhood Education.* New York: Macmillan, 1974.

Discusses application of socialization theory to early childhood curriculum.

824. Murphy, Lois B., and Leeper, Ethel M. *From "I" to "We."* OCD 74-1033. Washington, D.C.: U.S. Department of Health, Education, and Welfare, Bureau of Child Development Services, 1974.

Discusses attaining competence in early childhood and its pitfalls. Contains practical recommendations.

825. Orlick, Terry. *Winning Through Cooperation*. Washington, D.C.: Acropolis Books, 1978.

Differentiates between cooperative and competitive types of competition.

826. Piaget, Jean. *Language and Thought of the Child*. New York: The World Publishing Company, 1955.

Sees social interaction, conflicts, and arguments as the mechanics that free a child from egocentricity.

827. Read, Katherine, and Patterson, June. *The Nursery School and Kindergarten: Human Relationships and Learning*. 7th ed. New York: Holt, Rinehart, & Winston, 1980.

Discusses group relations in preschool and their meaning for the individual child. Gives helpful advice to teachers.

828. Redl, Fritz, and Wattenberg, William. *Mental Hygiene for Teachers*. New York: Harcourt Brace & World, 1959.

Educational classic that presents the strengths and pitfalls of group interaction.

829. ———. *When We Deal with Children*. New York: Free Press, 1966.

A collection of Redl's articles, many of which deal with group life.

830. Richards, Martin P. M., ed. *The Integration of a Child into a Social World*. Cambridge, England: Cambridge University Press, 1974.

Follows the process through which an infant develops into a competent member of society. Articles focus on biological, psychological and sociological viewpoints.

831. Roedell, Wendy Conklin; Slaby, R. G.; and Robinson, Halbert B. *Social Development in Young Children*. Washington, D.C.: National Institute of Education, U.S. Department of Health, Education, and Welfare, 1976.

Analysis of ways children acquire social skills.

832. Rubin, Zick. *Children's Friendships*. Cambridge, Mass.: Harvard University Press, 1980.

Examines the effect of the peer group on children's growing concept of friendships.

833. Schmuck, Richard A., and Schmuck, Patricia A. *Group Process*

in the Classroom. 3rd ed. Dubuque, Iowa: William C. Brown, 1979.

Describes differences in classroom climates and the influence of the teacher, and finds that a positive climate leads to mutual support and liking by students.

834. Schutz, Will. *Profound Simplicity*. New York: Bantam Books, 1979.

Sees social relationships developing in three stages beginning with "inclusion" which implies mutual recognition through "control," a mutual testing of power and mutual respect to "affection," a need to feel lovable and loving.

835. Selman, Robert. *The Growth of Interpersonal Understanding*. New York: Academic Press, 1980.

Examines children's social thinking on a developmental basis and finds that conflict resolution progresses on five levels, the first two of which fall within the early childhood range. Level 0 calls for physical solutions; Level 1 produces unrelated solutions, where children can still not conceptualize two conflicting points of view.

836. Smith, Charles A. *Promoting the Social Development of Young Children: Strategies and Activities*. Palo Alto, Calif.: Mayfield Publishing Company, 1982.

Provides many suggestions that can improve social interaction and overcome isolation and rejection through resolution of conflict in early childhood groups.

837. Turner, Marion E. *The Child Within the Group: An Experiment in Self-Government*. Stanford, Calif.: Stanford University Press, 1957.

This historic project proved that preschoolers can solve problems by developing a structure that leads to self-designed rules.

838. Webb, Roger A., ed. *Social Development in Childhood: Day Care Programs and Research*. Baltimore, Md.: The Johns Hopkins University Press, 1977.

A collection of papers exploring social development of toddlers and preschoolers as it is affected by mother-child attachment, by role playing and role taking, and the connections between intellectual and socio-emotional development.

839. Youniss, James. *Parents and Peers in Social Development*. Chicago: University of Chicago Press, 1980.

Finds that children's social relationship with adults is "complementary" (without initiative), while with peers it is characterized by "symmetrical reciprocity."

Studies and Articles

840. Apolloni, Tony, and Cooke, Thomas P. "Socially Withdrawn Children: The Role of Mental Health Practitioners." *Social Behavior and Personality* 5 (1977):337–341.

Reviews the literature regarding social withdrawal in childhood. Consideration is offered of the significance of the problem as an entity and as it is related to other patterns of maladaptive behavior. Classroom procedures which have proven effective in remediating social withdrawal are critically reviewed.

841. Ainsworth, Mary D. S. "The Development of Infant-Mother Attachment." In *Child Development and Social Policy: Review of Child Development Research*, edited by Bettye M. Caldwell and Henry N. Ricciuti, Vol. 3., pp. 1–94. Chicago: University of Chicago Press, 1973.

Found that children who were most anxious when separated from their mothers were those who were insecure in their relationships.

842. ———; Bell, Silvia M.; and Stayton, Donelda J. "Infant-Mother Attachment and Social Development: Socialization as a Product of Responsiveness to Signals." In *The Integration of a Child into a Social World*, edited by Martin P. M. Richards, pp. 99–135. Cambridge, England: Cambridge University Press, 1974.

Describes the development of social responsiveness in the infant as it is affected by the mother's style and sensitivity.

843. Bakeman, Roger, and Brownlee, John R. "The Strategy of Parallel Play: A Sequential Analysis." *Child Development* 51 (1980):873–878.

Concludes that the movement from parallel to group play in toddlers may be more a matter of minutes than months.

844. Belsky, Jay, and Steinberg, Lawrence D. "The Effects of Day Care: A Critical Review." *Child Development* 49 (1978):929–949.

Examines past studies and concludes that day care does not disrupt the mother-child bond and benefits the child's social development.

845. Bennings, Jaques S., and Crum, Ruth Ann. "'Acting Out' for Social Understanding." *Childhood Education* 58 (1982): 144–148.

Suggests that preschoolers can be helped to develop empathy through dramatic play and by listening to stories.

846. Bizman, Aharon; Yinon, Yoel; Mirtzari, Esther; and Shavit, Rivka. "Effects of the Age Structure of the Kindergarten on the Altruistic Behavior." *Journal of School Psychology* 16 (1978):154–159.

Found that children who were studying in heterogeneous (mixed-age) classes were more altruistic than were children from homogeneous classes.

847. Black, Janet K. "Are Young Children Really Egocentric?" *Young Children* 36 (1981):51–55.

Finds that when the context is meaningful and the situation real and basically human, young children are less egocentric than Piaget contends.

848. ———. "The Documentation of Kindergarten Children's Interactional Competency in an Informal Context of the Classroom." ERIC Document Reproduction Service, ED 191 547, 1980.

Studies sociodramatic play in a kindergarten classroom. Found that the children demonstrated (1) the ability to adapt to changes in the communicative setting; (2) they indicated the ability to use nonverbal behavior; (3) the children demonstrated familiarity with normal constraints and conditions of conversation; (4) they demonstrated the ability to sequence.

849. Blehar, Mary Curtis. "Anxious Attachment and Defensive Reactions Associated with Day Care." *Child Development* 45 (1974):683–692.

Compared the response to a strange situation of two and three year olds attending day care with that of home-reared children, and found that the latter group behaved with more assurance and less anxiety. This might indicate impairment of attachment in the day care groups.

850. Bryan, James H. "Children's Cooperation and Helping Behaviors." In *Review of Child Development and Research*, edited by E. Mavis Hetherington, Vol. 5., pp. 127–181. Chicago: The University of Chicago Press, 1975.

Cites studies that found preschoolers more cooperative and less competitive than older children, while older children tend to be more helpful than younger ones.

851. Bryant, Brenda K., and Crockenberg, Susan B. "Correlates and Dimensions of Prosocial Behavior: A Study of Female Siblings with Their Mothers." *Child Development* 51 (1980):529–544.

Investigates the maternal, sibling, and situational correlates of prosocial behavior between siblings and the relationship of prosocial to antisocial behavior.

852. Butler, Annie L. "Today's Child: Tomorrow's World." *Young Children* 32 (1976):4–11.

Discusses the role of education in preparing children for an unforeseeable future. Emphasizes needs for coping skills and creative resources to find answers and solutions as well as the importance of a positive self image that will facilitate group-oriented collaboration.

853. Castle, Kathryn S., and Richards, Herbert C. "Adult/Peer Interactions and Role Taking Ability Among Preschool Children." ERIC Document Reproduction Service, ED 156 337, 1978.

Found that preschoolers who interacted more with others were better able to take the role of others in dramatic play.

854. Corsaro, William A. "We're Friends, Right?: Children's

Use of Access Rituals in a Nursery School." *Language in Society* 8 (1979):315–336.

Found that preschoolers who wished to be included in a play activity were most successful if they displayed a similar activity, least successful when they were disruptive and they were not accepted when trying to intrude.

855. Cuffaro, Harriet K. "Dramatic Play: The Experience of Block Building." In *The Block Book*, edited by Elisabeth S. Hirsch, pp. 69–87. Washington, D.C.: National Association for the Education of Young Children, 1974.

Describes the reduction of egocentricity and ability to distance from oneself that occurs through preschool block-building activities. Children learn to comprehend the frame of reference of others, to define themselves in relation to the social world, to externalize and to symbolize their growing understanding of social relationships and of the community.

856. Dodge, Kenneth A. "Social Competence and Aggressive Behavior in Children." ERIC Document Reproduction Service, ED 202 584, 1981.

Found that aggressive boys are more likely than non-aggressive boys to interpret a peer as hostile and to act in hostile ways, and that selective recall of hostile cues is a significant predictor, or mediator, of an interpretation of peer hostility.

857. Eron, Leonard D. "Prescription for Reduction of Aggression." *American Psychologist* 35 (1980):244–252.

Reviews the results of a longitudinal study on socialization and child aggression. Proposes that boys be exposed to the same training that girls have traditionally received, and that they be encouraged to develop similar socially positive, nurturant, and sensitive qualities that are antithetical to aggressive behavior.

858. Finkelstein, Neal W.; Dent, Cathy; Gallacher, Kathleen; and Ramey, Craig T. "Social Behavior of Infants and Toddlers in a Day Care Environment." *Developmental Psychology* 14 (1978):257–262.

Found that as children become more mature, peer interaction increases and teacher-child interactions decrease.

859. Freud, Anna. "The Emotional and Social Development of Young Children." In *Feelings and Learning*, edited by Margaret Rasmussen, pp. 41–47. Washington, D.C.: Association for Childhood Education International, 1965.

Posits four stages in social development: (1) the child and the mother are a unit; (2) the child becomes interested in others as objects; (3) children can cooperate in a joint activity; and (4) other children can be valued in their own right.

860. Furman, Wyndol; Rahe, Donald; and Hartup, Willard W. "Rehabilitation of Socially Withdrawn Preschool Children Through Mixed-Aged and Same-Sex Socialization." *Child Development* 50 (1979):915–922.

Found that shyness and social isolation decrease when children had opportunities to play alone with younger playmates.

861. Garvey, Catherine, and Hogan, Robert. "Social Speech and Social Interaction: Egocentrism Revisited." *Child Development* 44 (1973):562–568.

Found that children aged 3½–5 years of age exhibited social speech and interpersonal understanding.

862. Gottman, John; Gonso, Jonni; and Rasmussen, Brian. "Social Interaction, Social Competence, and Friendship in Children." *Child Development* 46 (1975):709–718.

Found that peer relations affected children's ability to take the view of another.

863. Gray, Dianne Elaine. "The Teacher's Role in Understanding Aggression and Dealing with It Effectively in the Preschool Environment." ERIC Document Reproduction Service, ED 200 334, 1981.

Explores the role of the preschool teacher in dealing effectively with aggression in the classroom setting. Preventive and interventive approaches to dealing with aggression are suggested, including the control of space and room arrangement, the control of time, and the reinforcement of altruistic and appropriate behaviors. Intervention approaches advocated include emotional release through physical activities, the controlled use of sound to direct emotional states, and dramatic play. Ways for leading non-playing aggressive children toward participation in social play are described.

864. Greif, Esther Blank. "Peer Interaction in Preschool Children." In *Social Development in Childhood: Day Care Programs and Research*, edited by Roger A. Webb, pp. 141–160. Baltimore, Md.: The Johns Hopkins University Press, 1977.

Found that peer interaction facilitates and expedites social development in preschoolers.

865. Hallinan, Maureen T. "Friendship Patterns in Open and Traditional Classrooms." *Sociology of Education* 49 (1976): 254–265.

Found that open classrooms had fewer "social isolates," and fewer "stars" than traditional classes.

866. Hartup, Willard W. "Peer Relations: Developmental Implications and Interaction in Same- and Mixed-Age Situations." *Young Children* 32 (1977):4–13.

Compares social interaction in same-aged and mixed-age groups and concludes that both have valuable, albeit different influences on development.

867. Harwell, Helen B., and Harwell, John E. "An Exploratory Study of Social Values in Kindergartens." *Journal of the International Association of Pupil Personnel Workers* 25 (1981): 116–123.

Half the kindergarten children studied lacked leadership ability and appeared to be followers. Many lacked initiative, intellectual curiosity, and the ability to take constructive criticism. The authors suggest that schools have a responsibility to provide an environment free from deprivation of social values and urge that internal self-discipline replace external discipline.

868. Hirsch, Elisabeth S. "Reaction II to Bernard Spodek's 'Social Studies for Young Children: Identifying Intellectual Goals.'" *Social Education* 38 (1974):47–49.

Discusses the variety of ways preschool experience facilitates decentering. Children become less egocentric through (1) dramatic play, (2) social interaction and co-operation, (3) field trips, (4) representational activities such as art and blockbuilding, (5) listening to stories, (6) teachers' modeling of acceptance of individual differences and clarifying the feelings of others.

869. Hoffman, Martin L. "Developmental Synthesis of Affect and Cognition and Its Implications for Altruistic Motivation." *Developmental Psychology* 11 (1975):607–622.

Suggests three stages of responding to distress: Infants and toddlers respond sympathetically through identification; preschoolers and kindergartners begin to see the world through the other person's eyes; beginning with early grades children are able to take the personality into account.

870. Johnson, James E.; Yu, Sharon; and Roopnarine, Jaipul. "Social Cognitive Ability, Interpersonal Behaviors, and Peer Status Within a Mixed Age Group." ERIC Document Reproduction Service ED 196 520, 1980.

Found that children, aged 3–8 years, who suggested nonforceful strategies for solving interpersonal conflicts were most likely to be nominated as liked peers. Popular children tended to boss, teach and help. They had good communication ability and solved social problems by asking and helping. Disliked children tended to be followers and imitators.

871. Kohlberg, Lawrence. "Stage and Sequence: The Cognitive Developmental Approach to Socialization." In *Handbook of Socialization: Theory and Research*, edited by David H. Goslin, pp. 347–480. Chicago: Rand McNally, 1969.

Emphasizes the baby's natural desire to take part in social communication and to play with others. For most humans, the first playmate is the mother.

872. Lee, Lee C. "Toward a Cognitive Theory of Interpersonal Development: Importance of Peers." In *The Origins of Behavior*. Vol. 4: *Friendship and Peer Relations*, edited by Michael Lewis and Leonard A. Rosenblum, pp. 204–221. New York: John Wiley & Sons, 1975.

Describes the development of social cognition and interpersonal competence through the construction of social schemata.

873. Lewis, Michael; Young, Gerald; Brooks, Jeanne; and Michaelson, Linda. "The Beginning of Friendship." In *Friendship and Peer Relations*, edited by Michael Lewis and Leonard A. Rosenblum, pp. 27–66. New York: John Wiley & Sons, 1975.

Found that toddlers respond to strange adults more negatively than to strange peers.

874. Lieberman, A. F. "Preschoolers' Competence with a Peer: Relations with Attachment and Peer Experience." *Child Development* 48 (1977).

Found that three year olds, secure in their attachment to their mothers, had a positive orientation to other children.

875. Longee, Michael D.; Gruenreich, Royal; and Hartup, Willard. "Social Interaction in Same and Mixed-Age Dyads of Preschool Children." *Child Development* 48 (1977):1353–1361.

Observed that in mixed age dyads, children strive to adjust to their partners' level of maturity.

876. Maccoby, Eleanor E., and Jacklin, Carol Nagy. "Sex Differences in Aggression: A Rejoinder and Reprise." *Child Development* 53 (1980):964–980.

Presents evidence from cross-cultural studies and observational studies that support the contentions that males are more aggressive than females and that this sex difference is evident as early as the preschool years.

877. ———, and Masters, John. "Attachment and Dependency." In *Carmichaels Manual of Child Psychology*, edited by Paul Mussen, Vol. 2., pp. 73–157. New York: John Wiley & Sons, 1970.

Maintain that by age three or four early attachment becomes differentiated into proximity-seeking and attention-seeking directed at different people.

878. Macrae, John W., and Herbert-Jackson, Emily H. "Are Behavioral Effects of Infant Day Care Programs Specific?" *Developmental Psychology* 12 (1976):269–270.

Found that the peer relations of two year olds improved with prolonged day care experience.

879. Marcus, Robert F., and Leiserson, Marion. "Encouraging Helping Behavior." *Young Children* 33 (1978):24–34.

Describes ways in which prosocial behavior in preschool can be encouraged through classroom climate and structure, teacher modeling, and activities.

880. McCandless, Boyd R.; Bilous, Carolyn B.; and Bennett, Hanna L. "Peer Popularity and Dependence on Adults in Preschool Age Socialization." *Child Development* 32 (1961):511–518.

Found that children frequently in need of emotional support are less popular with their peers.

881. Moore, Shirley G. "Social Cognition: Knowing About Others." *Young Children* 34 (1979):54–61.

Reviews recent studies on the development of the ability to understand others. Finds role-taking activities important in the development of social competence.

882. Mueller, Edward, and Lucas, Thomas. "A Developmental Analysis of Peer Interaction Among Toddlers." In *Friendship and Peer Relations*, edited by Michael Lewis and Leonard Rosenblum, pp. 223–257. New York: John Wiley & Sons, 1975.

Show how children develop from being centered on physical objects through simple and complex social interchanges to complementary interchanges in one-to-one relations.

883. Nicolaysen, Mary. "Dominion in Children's Play: Its Meaning and Management." In *Ideas That Work with Young Children*, edited by Katherine Read Baker, pp. 167–175. Washington, D.C.: National Association for the Education of Young Children, 1972.

Children's possessiveness reflects their need to establish themselves as individuals, to achieve security and mastery. Only then can they move on to consider the needs of others.

884. Raph, Jane B.; Thomas, Alexander; and Chess, Stella. "The Influence of Nursery School on Social Interaction." *American Journal of Orthopsychiatry* 38 (1968):144–152.

Children's interaction increased with age. Negative interactions with children decreased with length of attendance; however, negative interactions with teachers increased.

885. Retish, Paul M. "Changing the Status of Poorly Esteemed Students Through Teacher Reinforcement." *Journal of Applied Behavioral Science* 9 (1973):44–50.

Found that if teachers helped students to be socially accepted their academic performance improved.

886. Rosenham, David. "The Kindness of Children." *Young Children* 25 (1969):30–44.

887. ———. "Prosocial Behavior of Children." In *The Young Child: Reviews and Research,* edited by Willard Hartup, pp. 340–359. Vol. 2. Washington, D.C.: National Association for the Education of Young Children, 1972.

Finds that young children are able to be kind either because they feel it is expected or because they reciprocate kindness.

888. Rubin, Zick. "What Is a Friend?" In *Readings in Developmental Psychology,* edited by Judith Krieger Gardener, pp. 236–243. 2d ed. Boston: Little Brown, 1982.

Finds that the peer group can help children to develop social skills as well as self-understanding and a sense of group belonging.

889. Rutherfod, Eldred, and Mussen, Paul H. "Generosity in Nursery School Boys." *Child Development* 39 (1968): 755–765.

Found that highly competitive boys were less likely to be generous.

890. Selman, Robert L., and Byrne, Diane F. "A Structural Developmental Analysis of Role Taking in Middle Childhood." *Child Development* 45 (1974):803–806.

Identified four stages of social perspective taking: egocentric, subjective, self-reflective, and mutual. The first two fall within early childhood range.

891. ———. "Toward a Structural Analysis of Developing Interpersonal Relations Concepts: Research with Normal and Disturbed Preadolescent Boys." In *Minnesota*

Symposium on Child Psychology, edited by Anne D. Pick, pp. 156–200. Vol. 10. Minneapolis, Minn.: University of Minnesota Press, 1976.

892. ———, and Jaquette, Dan. "Stability and Oscillation in Interpersonal Awareness: A Clinical Development Analysis." In *Nebraska Symposium on Motivation, 1977*, edited by Charles B. Keasy, pp. 261–304. Lincoln, Neb.: University of Nebraska Press, 1978.

893. ———, and Selman, Anne P. "Children's Ideas About Friendship: A New Theory." *Psychology Today*, 13 October 1979, pp. 71–114.

Identifies five stages in the development of friendships. The first two, "momentary partnership" and "friendship as a one-way assistance," fall within the range of early childhood.

894. Shantz, Carolyn Uhlinger. "The Development of Social Cognition." In *Review of Child Development Research*, edited by E. Mavis Hetherington, pp. 257–323. Vol. 5. Chicago: University of Chicago Press, 1975.

Examines the development of the ability to decenter and to make accurate inferences about the emotions, intentions, and thoughts of others during preschool years.

895. Shantz, David W., and Schomer, Joyce. "Interpersonal Conflict in Preschoolers: A Naturalistic Observation Study." ERIC Document Reproduction Services, ED 154 917, 1978.

Territory disputes were found to be more aggression prone than either interpersonal control or possession disputes among preschoolers.

896. Sharabany, Ruth, and Hertz-Lazarowitz, Rachel. "Do Friends Share and Communicate More than Non-Friends?" *International Journal of Behavioral Development* 4 (1981):45–59.

Found that among kindergarten and first-grade children, friends exhibited less sharing and communicative behaviors and more task relevant behaviors.

897. Sherman, Lawrence W. "An Ecological Study of Glee in Small Groups of Preschool Children." *Child Development* 46 (1975):53–61.

Presents a description and analysis of group glee (joyful screaming, laughing and intense physical acts occurring in simultaneous bursts or in a contagious fashion), its occurrence, location, frequency and duration, teachers' responses, incidence of disruption, and initiating causes.

898. Sluckin, Andrew M., and Smith, Peter K. "Two Approaches to the Concept of Dominance in Preschool Children." *Child Development* 48 (1977):917–923.

Found that preschool children established hierarchies based on perceived toughness.

899. Smith, Peter K. "A Longitudinal Study of Social Participation in Preschool Children: Solitary and Parallel Play Reexamined." *Developmental Psychology* 14 (1978):517–523.

Observed that group play increased and solitary play decreased during the nine-month period children were studied, while parallel play did not vary much in overall occurrence.

900. Sroufe, L. Alan. "Attachment and the Roots of Competence." *Human Nature*, October 1978. Reprinted in *Human Development 82/83*, edited by Hiram E. Fitzgerald and Thomas H. Carr, pp. 94–98. Guilford, Conn.: The Dushkin Publishing Group, 1982.

Found that 15 month olds with secure attachments to their primary caregivers became competent, successful, and autonomous toddlers.

901. Staub, Erwin. "Socialization by Parents and Peers and Experiential Learning of Prosocial Behavior." In *Mother/Child, Father/Child Relationships*, edited by Joseph H. Stevens, Jr. and Marilyn Matthews, pp. 69–82. Washington, D. C.: The National Association for the Education of Young Children, 1978.

Found that children behave in ways others behave toward them and that, conversely, peers will respond in ways that are similar to the behavior the individual directs to them.

902. Strayer, Floyd F. "Child Ethology and the Study of Preschool Social Relations." In *Friendship and Social Relations in Children*, edited by Hugh C. Foot, Anthony J. Chap-

man, and Jean R. Smith, pp. 235–265. New York: John Wiley & Sons, 1980.

Examines social conflict and dominance relations, affiliative activity and cohesive bonds; and prosocial activity and altruistic relations in preschool children.

903. Suls, Jerry, and Kalle, Robert. "Children's Moral Judgments as a Function of Intention, Damage, and an Actor's Physical Harm." *Developmental Psychology* 15 (1979):93–94.

Found that young children often believe in "immanent" justice, i.e., that the person who got hurt probably deserved it.

904. Tieger, Todd. "On the Biological Basis of Sex Differences in Aggression." *Child Development* 51 (1980):943–963.

Critically examines the empirical and theoretical basis for Maccoby and Jacklin's (876) contention that males are more biologically predisposed to aggressive behavior than are females.

905. White, Robert W. "Competence and the Psychosexual Stages of Development." In *The Causes of Behavior: Readings in Child Development and Educational Psychology*, edited by Judy F. Rosenblith and Wesley Allinsmith, pp. 300–308. Boston: Allyn & Bacon, 1966.

This influential article maintains that young children need a sense of competence in all phases of their lives, including the social world.

906. Wilson, Karl E., and Shantz, Carolyn Uhlinger. "Perceptual Role Taking Ability and Dependency Behavior in Preschool Children." *Merrill-Palmer Quarterly* 23 (1977): 205–211.

Found that perceptual role-taking ability in preschool children correlated positively with their dependency and attention-getting needs.

907. Yarrow, Marian R.; Scott, Phyllis M.; and Wexler, Carolyn Z. "Learning Concern for Others." *Developmental Psychology* 8 (1973):240–260.

908. ———, and Wexler, Carolyn Z. "Dimensions and Correlates of Prosocial Behavior in Young Children." *Child Development* 47 (1976):118–125.

Both studies examine the ability of 2–7 year olds to give, help, share, and comfort.

909. Yawkey, Thomas Daniels, and Fox, Frank D. "Evaluative Intervention Research in Child's Play. ERIC Document Reproduction Service, ED 197 831, 1980.

Reviews literature examining the potential of imaginative play to foster young children's cognitive and social development.

Books for Children

910. Asch, Frank. *The Last Puppy.* Englewood Cliffs, N.J.: Prentice-Hall, 1980.

Is it bad to be always last? A puppy finds that it can mean being special.

911. Baldwin, Anne Norris. *A Friend in the Park.* New York: Four Winds, 1973.

Eric and his mother have moved to Paris. The book depicts Eric's feelings of being left out because he does not know French. Eventually it is Eric who helps a new Portuguese girl.

912. Barkin, Carol, and James, Elizabeth. *Are We Still Best Friends?* Milwaukee, Wisc.: Raintree Editions, 1975.

Examines conflicting feelings that can arise in the course of friendship.

913. Binzen, Bill. *Carmen.* New York: Coward-McCann, 1969.

Depicts the frustration of a newly arrived Puerto Rican girl who eventually finds a friend.

914. Cohen, Miriam. *Will I Have a Friend?* New York: Collier, 1967.

Shows the experiences of a young child entering preschool in a new neighborhood.

915. Craig, Jean. *New Boy on the Sidewalk.* New York: W. W. Norton, 1967.

A boy has recently moved to a new neighborhood and makes a friend.

916. Dalton, Judy. *Two Good Friends*. New York: Crown Publishers, 1974.

    Warm friendship between a neat duck and a messy bear.

917. Grealish, Mary Jane Von Braunsberg, and Grealish, Charles A. *Amy Maura*. Syracuse, N.Y.: Human Policy Press, 1975.

    This simple, gentle story of a little girl with cerebral palsy should help all children to be sensitive and accepting toward the exceptional child, or for that matter, toward anyone who feels isolated and alone.

918. Kantrowitz, Mildred. *Good-bye Kitchen*. New York: Parents Magazine Press, 1972.

    Emily faces the loss of her friend who moves away.

919. Lobel, Arnold. *Frog and Toad Are Friends*. New York: Harper & Row, 1970.

920. ———. *Frog and Toad All Year*. New York: Harper & Row, 1979.

    Adventures of two very good friends.

921. Lystad, Mary. *That New Boy*. New York: Crown Publishers, 1973.

    George is unable to approach a newcomer and covers up his shyness by disdain.

922. Mannheim, Grete. *The Two Friends*. New York: Alfred A. Knopf, 1968.

    A little girl's shyness, fright, and loneliness on entering kindergarten are alleviated when she finds a friend.

923. Ormsby, Virginia H. *What's Wrong with Julio?* Philadelphia: J. B. Lippincot, 1965.

    The children in school are puzzled at Julio's distant behavior until they find out that he misses his parents. Then they decide to help him.

924. Robinson, Charles. *New Kid in Town*. New York: Atheneum, 1975.

    A new arrival is victimized by a bully but is able to assert himself.

925. Rogers, Fred. *Mister Rogers Talks About . . . .* New York: Platt & Munk, 1974.

Shows preparations prior to moving, such as fantasy play, and discusses ways of not losing contact with old friends and places.

926. Steig, William. *Amos and Boris.* New York: Farrar, Straus, & Giroux, 1971.

Amos, a mouse, and Boris, a whale, are very close friends. Whey they are forced to part, their relationship leaves a lasting effect.

927. Stein, Sara Bennett. *About Handicaps.* New York: Walker & Company, 1974.

Mathew reacts with fear and avoidance to Joe's "crooked legs." Mathew's father helps them to build a positive relationship.

928. Udry, Janice May. *Let's Be Enemies.* New York: Scholastic, 1961.

Even the best of friends have fights.

929. Wells, Rosemary. *Timothy Goes to School.* New York: Dial, 1981.

His first three days at school Timothy tries to make friends with the class perfectionist. But then he makes friends with Violet and begins to enjoy school.

930. Whitmore, Martha. *My Friend William Moved Away.* Nashville, Tenn.: Abingdon Press, 1979.

Jimmy is sad when his friend moves away, but then he finds a new friend.

931. Wolde, Gunilla. *Betsy's First Day at Nursery School.* New York: Random House, 1976.

Shows Betsy's beginning doubts, which are allayed when she makes a friend.

932. Yashima, Tara. *Crow Boy.* New York: Viking, 1955.

This book has become a classic. It depicts Chibi, a shy boy in rural Japan, who develops a special sensitivity to the sights and sounds around him. A sensitive teacher helps the other children to appreciate Chibi's special talents.

933. Zolotov, Charlotte. *The Three Funny Friends.* New York: Harper & Row, 1961.

A little girl who has moved recently finds that she can give up her three imaginary friends when she becomes friendly with the boy next door.

934. ———. *Janey.* New York: Harper & Row, 1973.

A young girl faces her feelings of loss as she remembers her friend who has moved away.

935. ———. *The Unfriendly Book.* New York: Harper & Row, 1975.

What is worse: To like everyone or to find fault with all? Bertha and Judy have a real confrontation.

STRONG FEELINGS

Life means growth. Emotional development parallels physical growth in many ways. In order to guide young children toward healthy maturity we must be aware of the process of emotional development and the many pitfalls along the way. This is the area where all concerned with the child's well-being should work together, so that children get a sense of sound and trustworthy support from the adult world.

Building a *sense of trust* is the child's first developmental task according to Erikson (941). Very young children, totally helpless, overwhelmed by their inner needs, can tolerate only very little frustration. Time goes very, very slowly for a young child. Waiting for a bottle for only five minutes seems to the child like waiting for hours. The infant needs a trustworthy, dependable world. Only if he develops faith in people can he allow himself to reach out to it.

The need for dependable trustworthy adults does not cease in babyhood. Entering preschool, for instance, causes a new crisis in confidence. Successful resolution of school adjustment provides the child with additional supportive, trustworthy adults.

Children will consider adults dependable if they feel protected by them. Such need for protection goes far beyond needs for creature comforts, however. Children need consistent policies and regular schedules (946). They need a sense of strength and dependability that will protect them against their own bad wishes and uncontrolled urges (942) as well as against real or imagined dangers. Only when they feel that their needs for

201

dependency are being met are they able to move on to new relationships with adults and children (960). Read and Patterson also emphasize that if children have failed to develop a sense of trust earlier, it will be the task of the teacher to provide the total acceptance they need in order to be able to enter into play and begin to benefit from school.

The second task of a healthy personality, according to Erikson, is to develop *a sense of autonomy that outweighs shame and doubt.* This struggle begins with the toddler. It includes the "NO" stage with its insistence on "me do it" and toilet training, so often a source of shame and humiliation. Children struggling with this stage need fair, judicious adults, who are not threatened by the contrary toddler and his rebellious assertion of selfhood. Again, the work of this stage will not be finished in the toddler years. Stubbornness, for instance, may have its source in the young child's insistence that he is *someone.* Children need many opportunities to do things for themselves and to make decisions at this age (946).

Gradually, as independence is strengthened the child becomes ready to grapple with the third stage, which Erikson calls *initiative versus guilt.* Children become even more active, exploring, investigating. Initiative, exploration, finding out the possibilities inherent in things and people is the basis of all cognitive development as well as of a sense of "I can do" that is the foundation of a sound self-image. This age (3–5) also contains the beginnings of a conscience. While a conscience is necessary and valuable, feeling too guilty can be paralyzing and make the child's controls break down (960). Children feeling too guilty for their misdeeds will fail to build confidence in themselves.

Fraiberg (942) differentiates carefully between guilt produced by a healthy personality and neurotic guilt feelings. "A child needs to feel our disapproval at certain times," she says, "but if our reaction is of such strength that he feels worthless and despised, we have abused our power. . . ."

Anna Freud (971) differentiates between fear and anxiety. Fear is the response to real danger, while anxiety is the result of a clash between drives and internal opposing forces. Children who are not yet in full control of their drives but are attempting to build up their conscience by internalizing the values of beloved adults are often victims of anxiety. In order to keep such anxiety at a tolerable level, says Freud, they often exchange internal anxiety for imaginary external threats. We are all familiar with fears of preschool children which pop up without sufficiently good reason and are resistant to reasonable arguments. What makes our arguments even more futile is the fact that preschool children are not yet clear on the difference between reality and fantasy (940). Piaget concurs in his description of the way children under five consider inanimate objects alive and dreams real (959).

Hirsch (948) describes the ways satisfying, meaningful activities in a preschool can keep anxiety at bay. Sudden change or particularly long waiting periods, however, bring anxiety to the fore. Children's behavior becomes more aggressive and more babyish. Aggression is often the result of unconscious fear. Many children feel that they live in a jungle and that danger lurks everywhere. "I hit him back first," explained a preschooler to me once. Such children will be able to become less defensive when they feel sufficiently protected by the adults and their anxiety becomes allayed through meaningful activities, which builds their inner strength and resistance. Aggression can have more immediate causes, too. Inconsistent expectations by adults, or even expectations the child considers unreasonable, a new baby at home, failure to get attention and response, harsh methods of adult control (960), all can provoke aggressive outbursts.

Preschool teachers know that individual children differ and need to be handled differently. Constant observation and remembering ways individual children respond, or failed to do so, will help teachers to learn from their own mistakes. Teachers need to remember that mistakes with individuals are unavoidable and do little harm. Repeating the same ineffective response, on the other hand, will only lead to frustration for all.

There are a few general guidelines that can be helpful to teachers. Hendrick (946) suggests that teachers should (1) analyze conditions leading to misbehavior and try to correct them; (2) be alert to potential behavior and try to correct before disaster strikes. (Since teachers cannot be everywhere at once, it is useful, in this connection, to be aware of noise levels. "Highness" of impending explosions has a clearly discernible, high-pitched sound.) (3) Teachers should convey a sense of warmth along with a sense of firmness. Read and Patterson (960) add that adults must also be in touch with their own hostile feelings. If we are able to accept children's hostility without reciprocating we will be able to convey to them that it is o.k. to *feel* angry—but not to *do* angry, hostile things.

Some children will react to anxiety and stress by regressing. In a sense we all do this. The well-traveled familiar path can give us comfort and security. In the same way the toddler who has just learned to walk will revert to crawling when in a hurry. Preschool children will wet their beds, whine, suck their thumbs, get comfort from masturbation, or from holding a "transitional object."

Some children, instead of hitting out against the world, draw back timidly. These children often get less attention than their aggressive or friendly, outgoing peers. Thus the shy child gets rebuffed by teachers and, usually, by peers as well. Shyness can result from anxiety and a sense of danger. It can be a sign of a poor self-image and lack of a sense of personal worth. Shy children often get along well with older people or with children much younger than themselves (960). Shyness can also be a sign of more serious disturbance. In any case, shyness should not be disregarded. The shy child needs the warming presence of a not-too-intrusive adult. Eventually a nonthreatening companion might ease the way into social and play activities.

Children's feelings can run the whole gamut of the scale from anger to affection, from happiness to deep sadness. Their feelings are deeper and more complex than the vocabulary at their disposal to express it. No wonder, then, that children so often reply "Nothing" to the teacher's concerned inquiry about what the matter is.

Children's behavior itself is often a form of cry for help and should be interpreted as such. Nonverbal clues to children's feelings are described by a number of authors (939, 960, 965).

Children can benefit from teachers verbalizing their feelings for them. While such language ought to be tentative lest it overwhelm the child, being given the opportunity—and the words—to express his feelings can be a great relief. Temper tantrums are often a child's way of showing adults how he feels. Providing him with a more acceptable and more mature way of expressing his feelings by saying "Your face tells me that you are very angry" will speed his growth toward socially acceptable behavior and inner controls.

Sometimes adults feel very uncomfortable in the presence of a sulky or sad child. Telling such children to "Let us see your smile" tells them that genuine expression of strong feelings is not acceptable, or—worse—that adults do not want to be bothered with their unhappiness.

Teachers are not psychologists. "There is a great value in teacher's understanding of the deep symbolism of the child's behavior," says Barbara Biber (968), "but it is not the teacher's role to become involved in these deep underlying processes. Instead, the teacher needs to be certain that the learning environment supplies opportunities for the children themselves to find outlets for expressing their feelings and symbolizing their fantasies."

A well-run early childhood program with a full range of expressive activities, art materials, blocks, dramatic play possibilities, music and movement, story telling, with opportunities for free choice, for experimenting and learning about things and people, can in most instances provide the support that helps children to strengthen their resistance to emotional hardship and thus master their difficulties.

BIBLIOGRAPHY

Books and Pamphlets for Adults

936. Berman, Louise M., and Roderick, Jessie A. *Feeling, Valuing, and the Art of Growing: Insights into the Affective.* Washington, D.C.: Association for Supervision and Curriculum Development, 1977.

    Presents an overview of the importance of the emotional side of education.

937. Bowlby, John. *Separation: Anxiety and Anger.* Vol. 2 of *Attachment and Loss.* New York: Basic Books, 1973.

    Examines behavioral indicators of fear and the kind of situations that elicit fear at different developmental stages.

938. Comer, James, and Poussaint, Alvin F. *Black Child Care: How to Bring up a Healthy Black Child in America.* New York: Pocket Books, 1975.

    Written in question-and-answer form, it gives understanding advice to parents who have to help black children to grow up healthy in a white society.

939. Despert, J. Louise. *The Inner Voices of Children.* New York: Bruner/Mazel, 1975.

    A collection of candid photographs with captions, examining nonverbal clues that might help adults to decipher the messages of children.

940. Elkind, David. *Children and Adolescents: Interpretive Essays on Jean Piaget.* 2d ed. New York: Oxford University Press, 1974.

Describes the confusion in preschoolers between symbol and referent, reality and fantasy.

941. Erikson, Erik H. *Childhood and Society*. Rev. ed. New York: Norton, 1964.

Describes stages of emotional development and the paramount importance of the resolution of each stage.

942. Fraiberg, Selma H. *The Magic Years: Understanding and Handling the Problems of Early Childhood*. New York: Charles Scribner's Sons, 1959.

This early childhood classic combines Freudian and Piagetian insights to help teachers and parents to understand the way children feel and think.

943. Freed, Alwyn M. *T.A. for Tots (and Other Prinzes)*. Sacramento, Calif.: Jalmar Press, 1973.

Introduction to transactional analysis that gives parents and children an easy vocabulary that might help them to communicate.

944. Ginott, Haim G. *Between Parent and Child: New Solution to Old Problems*. New York: Macmillan, 1965.

Offers many concrete suggestions that will help parents to determine their children's feelings and offers appropriate ways to respond.

945. Gould, Rosalind. *Child Studies Through Fantasy: Cognitive-Affective Patterns in Development*. New York: Quadrangle Books, 1972.

Finds that aggression and anxiety in preschoolers can be triggered by fluctuations of certainty about reality, fantasy, and reality within fantasy.

946. Hendrick, Joanne. *Total Learning for the Whole Child: Holistic Curriculum for Children Ages 2 to 5*. St. Louis, Mo.: C. V. Mosby, 1980.

Comprehensive chapter on the preschool's role in achieving emotional competence.

947. ———. *The Whole Child: New Trends in Early Education*. 2nd ed. St. Louis, Mo.: C. V. Mosby, 1980.

Discusses ways to establish a "therapeutic climate" in the preschool classroom that will allow children to build up their strengths in order to overcome their difficulties.

948. Hirsch, Elisabeth S. *Transition Periods: Stumbling Blocks of Education.* New York: Early Childhood Education Council, n.d.

Describes the rise of anxiety levels during periods of transition and resulting behavior problems. Gives suggestions to teachers.

949. Isaacs, Susan. *Troubles of Children and Parents.* New York: Schocken Books, 1973. (First published 1948.)

Contains answers to parents' questions on shyness, aggressiveness, fears, and anxieties.

950. Joint Commission on the Mental Health of Children. *Crisis in Child Mental Health: Challenge for the 1970's.* New York: Harper & Row, 1970.

Includes recommendations to Congress on improving child mental health and discusses the important role of day-care and preschool education.

951. Jones, Richard M. *Fantasy and Feeling in Education.* New York: New York University Press, 1968.

Shows that neglecting strong emotions aroused by educational material prevents children from reaping the full cognitive benefit.

952. Kellerman, Jonathan. *Helping the Fearful Child: A Guide to Everyday and Problem Anxieties.* New York: W. W. Norton, 1981.

Helpful answers to problems of parents faced with children's fears and anxieties. Provides clear distinction between "normal" fears and those that indicate need for professional help.

953. Lewis, Michael, and Rosenblum, Leonard A. *The Origins of Fear.* New York: John Wiley & Sons, 1974.

Examines the expression and development of fear in human infants in various settings. Also considers parallel phenomena in the behavior of animals.

954. Murphy, Lois, and Leeper, Ethel M. *The Ways Children Learn.* DHEW Publication OCD 73-1026. Washington, D.C.: U.S. Department of Health, Education, and Welfare, 1973.

Discusses the factors that help or hinder children's learning including the affective areas of trust, fear, anger, frustration, self-confidence, self-control, and the need for a supporting, loving teacher.

955. ———. *More than a Teacher*. DHEW Publication OCD 73-1027. Washington, D.C.: U.S. Department of Health, Education, and Welfare, 1973.

Discusses the teacher's role in fulfilling emotional needs of children.

956. ———. *Preparing for Change*. DHEW Publication OCD 73-1028. Washington, D.C.: U.S. Department of Health, Education, and Welfare, 1973.

Discusses the difficulties children experience when faced with change and the teacher's role in helping them.

957. ———. *Away from Bedlam*. DHEW Publication OCD 73-1029. Washington, D.C.: U.S. Department of Health, Education, and Welfare, 1973.

Discusses frustrations, fears, and anxieties that can arise in preschools due to frustration, anger, overstimulation, and contagion. Provides guidelines to prevent or handle disruptive situations.

958. Murphy, Lois Barclay, and Moriarty, Alice E. *Vulnerability, Coping and Growth from Infancy to Adolescence*. New Haven, Conn.: Yale University Press, 1976.

Examines personal resilience and vulnerability in the way children cope with stress.

959. Piaget, Jean. *The Child's Conception of the World*. Totowa, N.J.: Littlefield, Adams & Company, 1965.

Describes the way children under five years of age consider inanimate objects alive and dreams real.

960. Read, Katherine, and Patterson, June. *The Nursery School and Kindergarten: Human Relationships and Learning*. 7th ed. New York: Holt, Rinehart, & Winston, 1980.

Discusses feelings of hostility and aggression as expressed in school, their possible origins and ways in which adults can help.

961. Redl, Fritz, and Wattenberg, William. *Mental Hygiene in Teaching*. 2nd ed. New York: Harcourt, Brace & World, 1959.

    Educational classic that presents the concept of mental hygiene and ego support in the classroom. Contains a valuable chapter describing ways adults and children cope with emotional conflicts.

962. Warren, Rita M. *Caring: Supporting Children's Growth*. Washington, D.C.: National Association for the Education of Young Children, 1977.

    Discusses many issues dealing with mental health. Provides help for teachers in dealing with children in a growth-promoting and honest manner.

963. Wolman, Benjamin B. *Children's Fears*. New York: Grosset & Dunlap, 1978.

    This helpful book is organized in two ways. It presents fears developmentally, discussing fears that are usual at each age. The second section catalogues children's fears alphabetically, offering a brief description under each heading.

964. Zimbardo, Philip G., and Radl, Shirley. *The Shy Child: Overcoming and Preventing Shyness from Infancy to Adulthood*. New York: McGraw-Hill, 1981.

    Presents a program for conquering shyness in childhood and contains many suggestions for parents and teachers.

Studies and Articles

965. Ackerman, Paul, and Keppelman, Murray. "How to Understand Your Child's Distress Signals." *Redbook Magazine*, April 1979. Reprinted in *Early Childhood Education 80/81*, edited by Judy Spitler McKee, pp. 197–200. Guilford, Conn.: Dushkin Publishing Group, 1980.

    Describes nonverbal distress signals of children and their meanings. Offers helpful suggestions.

966. Bakke, Kit. "Anxiety and the 3–5 Year Old." *Day Care and Early Education*, Winter 1977. Reprinted in *Early Child-*

hood Education 80/81, edited by Judy Spitler McKee, pp. 194–196. Guilford, Conn.: Dushkin Publishing Group, 1980.

Discusses signs and causes of anxiety and offers suggestions on helping children to cope.

967. Berger, Alan S. "Anxiety in Young Children." *Young Children* 27 (1971):5–11.

Examines the young child's perceptions of danger and intolerable frustration, the causes and manifestations of fear and anxiety, and ways such feelings can be overcome.

968. Biber, Barbara. "Thinking and Feeling." *Young Children* 35 (1979): 4–16.

Deplores emphasis on cognitive development to the exclusion of affective growth. Urges a synthesis that will enhance children's development in all areas.

969. Butler, Annie L. "Dealing with Intense Feelings: Children and Crises." In *When There Is a Crisis: Helping Children Cope with Change,* edited by Sandra M. Long and Barbara Batchelor, pp. 1–11. Terre Haute, Ind.: Indiana Association for the Education of Young Children, 1979.

Discusses children's ability to comprehend crisis situations according to their developmental level. Gives guidelines for helping adults.

970. Freud, Anna. "Emotional and Social Development of Young Children." In *Feeling and Learning,* edited by Margaret Rasmussen, pp. 41–47. Washington, D.C.: Association for Childhood Education International, 1965.

Specifies four areas where children's mode of thinking and feeling differs from adults: (1) children see the world in an egocentric way; (2) child behavior governed by fears, wishes, impulses, and fantasies, even if reason is present; (3) children have a vastly different time sense; and (4) children translate facts connected with sex into crude, primitive, and brutal fantasies.

971. ———. "Fears, Anxieties, and Phobic Phenomena." In *Psychoanalytic Study of the Child,* pp. 85–90. Vol. 32. New Haven, Conn.: Yale University Press, 1977.

Differentiates between "fear" which is reaction to external danger and "anxiety," which is reaction to internal threats. Phobic responses can be defenses, protecting the child from trauma and panic caused by fear or anxiety.

972. Fried, Hilda. "'Plain Talk' About Dealing with the Angry Child." *Journal of the International Association of Pupil Personnel Workers* 25 (1981):17–21.

Parents and teachers must allow children to feel all their feelings, including anger. Children can be helped to accept their feelings and to channel and direct them to constructive ends. Discipline should be motivated by the need to protect and teach, not a desire to punish.

973. Furman, Wyndol; Rahe, Donald; and Hartup, Willard W. "Rehabilitation of Socially Withdrawn Preschool Children Through Mixed-Aged and Same-Sex Socialization." *Child Development* 50 (1979):915–922.

Found that shyness and social isolation decreased when children had opportunities to play alone with younger playmates.

974. Gardner, Dorothy E. M. "Emotions—A Basis for Learning." In *Feelings and Learning*, edited by Margaret Rasmussen, pp. 34–40. Washington, D.C.: Association for Childhood Education International, 1965.

Points out the essential connection between emotions and intellectual interests. Play, which is the child's way of learning gratifies wishes, expresses feelings, while at the same time children explore, experiment, imitate, ask questions, listen, and think.

975. Hooper, Laura. "Keeping in Step with Children." In *Feelings and Learning*, edited by Margaret Rasmussen, pp. 48–52. Washington, D.C.: Association for Childhood Education International, 1965.

Discusses the teacher's role in helping the individual. The hesitant child, the doubtful, the fearful, the confident, the far-out-in-front, all have different needs.

976. Hyson, Marion Carey. "Lobster on the Sidewalk: Understanding and Helping Children with Fears." *Young Children* 34 (1979):54–60.

Traces various stages of fearfulness in children by following ways they learn to interpret their world. Offers many suggestions.

977. Jenkins, Gladys Gardner. "For Parents Particularly (II)." *Childhood Education* 55 (1979):157–159.

This article addressed to parents identifies various causes of stress in young children, and delineates methods which can be used to help children to cope with stress.

978. Lourie, Reginald S., and Schwarzbeck, Charles. "When Children Feel Helpless in the Face of Stress." *Childhood Education* 55 (1979):134–140.

Describes the effect of various kinds of stresses on the organization of children's thinking, and the uniqueness of children's individual responses to these stresses.

979. Maurer, Adah. "What Children Fear." *The Journal of Genetic Psychology* 106 (1965):265–277.

Preschool children were found to be afraid of wild animals (mainly snakes, lions, and tigers) and imaginary beings, such as monsters.

980. Meathenia, Peggy Sue. "An Experience with Fear in the Lives of Children." *Childhood Education* 48 (1971):5–79.

Description of art experiences that helped children to overcome trauma caused by a tornado.

981. Murphy, Lois Barclay. "Feelings and Learning." In *Feelings and Learning*, edited by Margaret Rasmussen, pp. 26–33. Washington, D.C.: Association for Childhood Education International, 1965.

Warns that children can only be free for positive satisfactions and for learning for its own sake if they are not preoccupied with hunger, disappointment, anger, or fear.

982. Nagera, Humberto. "Sleep and Its Disturbances Approached Developmentally." In *The Psychoanalytic Study of the Child*, pp. 393–447. Vol. 21. New York: International Universities Press, 1966.

Discusses in detail cause for sleep disturbances at various levels of development. Considers sleep disturbances mainly signs of developmental disturbance.

983. Rohe, William, and Patterson, Arthur H. "The Effects of

Varied Levels of Resources and Density of Behavior in a Day Care Center." In *Man-Environment Interaction,* edited by D. H. Carson. Stroudsburg, Pa.: Hutchinson Ross, 1974.

Insufficient space to play, crowding and frustration resulted in more aggressive behavior.

984. Senn, Milton J. E. "Early Childhood Education for What Goals?" *Children* 16 (1969):8–13.

Deplores early childhood programs that focus on didactic teaching, distinctive stimulation, and premature emphasis on skills and neglect the emotional and social needs of children.

985. Smith, Peter K., and Conolly, K. J. "Social and Aggressive Behavior in Preschool Children as a Function of Crowding." *Social Science Information* 16 (1976):601–620.

Found that aggressive behavior in preschoolers increased when there was not enough space and too few materials.

986. ———. "Social and Situational Determinants of Fear in the Playgroup." In *The Origins of Fear,* edited by Michael Lewis and Leonard A. Rosenblum, pp. 107–129. New York: John Wiley & Sons, 1974.

Examines fear reactions in a preschool group as the result of novel or unexpected situations and as the result of crowding.

Books for Children

987. Beckman, Kaj. *Lisa Cannot Sleep.* New York: Franklin Watts, 1969.

Lisa insists on her favorite toys, one after another, to keep her company in bed.

988. Brown, Margaret Wise. *Goodnight Moon.* New York: Harper & Row, 1947.

An early childhood classic that offers a gentle transition from day to night.

989. Brown, Myra B. *Benji's Blanket.* New York: Franklin Watts, 1962.

Benji's "transitional object" accompanies him everywhere until he realizes that he is ready to manage without it.

990. Feder, Jane. *The Night-Light*. New York: Dial, 1980.

Reassuring book for children afraid of the dark. Kate explores various options to find one that is effective for her.

991. Hazen, Nancy. *Grownups Cry, Too/Los Adultos Tambien Lloran*. Chapel Hill, N.C.: Lollipop Power, 1973.

Accepts honest expression of emotion as appropriate. Written in English and Spanish.

992. Krasilovsky, Phyllis. *Scaredy Cat*. New York: Macmillan, 1959.

A little kitten is scared of many things.

993. Kraus, Robert. *Goodnight Richard Rabbit*. New York: Springfellow Books and E. P. Dutton, 1972.

A small rabbit calls his mother again and again because he is afraid of various fantasy animals. His mother is reassuring but firm.

994. Kross, Steven. *That Makes Me Mad!* New York: Pantheon, 1976.

Depicts everyday irritations children will recognize.

995. Lund, Doris Herold. *Did You Ever Dream?* New York: Parents Magazine Press, 1969.

Provides an opportunity for 5–8 year olds to separate dreams from reality.

996. Mayer, Mercer. *There's a Nightmare in My Closet*. New York: Dial Press, 1968.

Sensitive and funny, this acknowledges that nightmares are scary—even if they are silly.

997. Schlein, Miriam. *The Way Mothers Are*. Chicago: Albert Whitman, 1963.

Emphasizes that mothers love their children, no matter what.

998. Showers, Paul. *A Book of Scary Things*. Garden City, N.Y.: Doubleday, 1977.

Gives a humorous view of fear—adults' and children's, real and imaginary.

999. Stein, Sara Bonnett. *About Phobias: An Open Family Book for Parents and Children Together*. New York: Walker & Company, 1979.

Dual narrative, one for children, the other for the parent or teacher, is helpful in discussing fears, anxieties, and phobias. Written in consultation with the Center for Preventive Psychiatry.

1000. Watson, Jane Werner; Switzer, Robert E.; and Hirschberg, Cotter J. *Sometimes I'm Afraid: Sometimes I'm Angry: Read-Together-Books for Parents and Children*. Created in cooperation with the Menninger Foundation. New York: Golden Press, 1971.

Both books deal with strong feelings and help parents to discuss these emotions with their children.

WHEN DO CHILDREN NEED SPECIAL HELP?
HOW DO YOU GET IT?

The decision to get outside professional help occurs in all contingencies of our daily lives. We often resist calling the plumber, going to a lawyer or consulting a doctor, feeling that we should have been able to help ourselves and that depending on an outsider somehow diminishes our self-sufficiency.

Getting help when emotional problems occur has an additional component. For many people it means an acceptance of problems that by this very acceptance become more real. Parents also may feel that the professional they consult may blame them, that if they only had handled things better, their child's development would have gone more smoothly. They have read articles or heard talks that describe parent-child relations in a simplistic cause-and-effect way. In actual fact babies are born with their own peculiarities that may even affect their parents' ways of responding to them. The parent-child unit does not live in a sealed environment, unaffected by the outside world. Parents have to contend with a great many realities, social and economic factors, world events, environmental influences, friends, relations, relationships within their intimate family, and factors inherent in their own and their children's psychological make-up. Professionals, well aware of these factors, are more likely to offer sympathy than to cast blame.

Most parents have wondered at one time or another, whether their child's behavior is just part of the normal process of growing up or whether it should give reason for concern. A certain amount of stress and turmoil is unavoidable and even necessary to mental health, just as developing immunities is important for physical well-being. Parents often have to decide whether to take children to a doctor or clinic, or to trust that their physical problems will cure themselves with some rest, simple home remedies, and an extra dose of tender loving care. In the same way some emotional upheavals will be "self-terminating" while others should be considered as signs which require additional help. Early childhood years are usually considered particularly auspicious for early intervention for mental health problems. Children are open and available at this age. They have not yet built up the complex defenses of the older child and adult.

How do we know when to reach out for help? An initial visit to the clinic or physician who knows the child might be a wise first step. Preschool teachers and directors often can give a more detached and objective report on the child. Parents feeling concerned might wish to go for an initial diagnostic evaluation, even if they are not at all sure that outside help is really necessary. Such a "check-up" will reassure them if there is no cause for concern. On the other hand, it will provide them with an opportunity to get suggestions for further steps, if that seems indicated. Such diagnostic evaluation can be obtained in most clinics and mental health centers. If individual practitioners are consulted it may be wise to go to persons well known in their field of competence. Even if they are unable to continue with the child, they can suggest others particularly suited to the child, the parents and the problem at hand.

Parents (or teachers) can be aware of various symptoms that may be signals of difficulty. Note, however, that one symptom alone rarely spells trouble. It might, however, give us a warning to be on the lookout for other signals.

Mayer and Hoover (1003) give the following helpful list of danger signals:

From birth to two years, slow physical development, excessive passivity, lack of responsiveness, excessive restlessness, difficulties in sleeping or eating.

From two to four years, frequent night terrors; severe eating difficulties; constant insistence on a bottle instead of a glass or cup; refusal to begin toilet training; refusal to accept any limits on behavior; marked lack of interest in other children, especially toward the end of this period; inability to let the mother out of sight without signs of panic; panic (not just shyness) when approached by strangers.

From four to six years, inability to get along with children, constant fighting or anxious withdrawal; repeated and intentional cruelty to animals; constant destructiveness; intense, frequent temper tantrums with no obvious provocation; continuing unwillingness to be separated from mother; *intense* fears of *many* things; consistent day or night wetting or soiling; stuttering or other poor speech; tics—involuntary movements of face or body parts; inability or unwillingness to do things for himself.

From six to eight years, absorption in fantasies, treated as if they were real; school phobia—anxiety attacks in the morning, vomiting, stomach ache, etc., without physical cause; continuous bedwetting and thumbsucking, frequent masturbation in public (*not* just when alone); inability to follow directions in school, failure to show a beginning interest in learning; intense worry about becoming ill, fears of bodily injury, psychosomatic symptoms, i.e., vomiting, stomach-ache, diarrhoea, headache, etc., without physical cause; pronounced fear of elevators, crossing the street, being alone in a room, constant, intense fear of the dark.

Mayer and Hoofer suggest that parents try to size up the total picture before coming to a conclusion, by asking themselves (1) is the child's behavior generally appropriate to the circumstances in which he finds himself; (2) is the child's behavior generally in keeping with his age; (3) are there real difficulties in the child's environment that may be to blame for the problem; (4) has there been a radical change in the child's behavior; and (5) how long has the symptom lasted?

Jonathan Kellerman (1002) lists, in addition, a number of experiences that might be stress producing for children, such as hospitalization, divorce, or death in the family. If children show behavior change after such disturbing experiences it certainly should be discussed with a competent professional.

Charles Shaw's book (1004) describes major disorders, childhood schizophrenia, brain damage, psychoneurosis, psychopathy, learning disabilities, personality disorder and mental retardation. These disturbances are beyond the scope of the present volume. The reference is included as an informational resource.

Finding Professional Help

As mentioned earlier, the family physician, pediatrician, or pediatric clinic usually caring for the child might be the ones who not only suggest what kind of treatment is needed and who is best qualified to provide it, they will also establish the contact, "make the referral."

Another way to obtain referral is to go to a Family Service Agency. If there is no such listing in the telephone book, the local United Fund or Community Chest may be of help. Child Guidance Clinics are often helpful. They usually are affiliated with universities, hospitals and school departments.

Other sources may be obtained from the State Department of Health or Mental Health. Local general hospitals or mental hospitals often have outpatient clinics.

Information can be obtained also from the National Mental Health Association, 1800 North Kent Street, Rosslyn Station, Arlington, Virginia 22209, and The National Black Child Development Institute, 1463 Rhode Island Avenue, N.W., Washington, D.C. 20002. In many localities these organizations have local chapters.

There are a variety of professions whose members understand children and can treat their emotional problems: psychiatrists, psychoanalysts, psychologists, play therapists, social workers. In clinics and social agencies often a team composed of several of these professionals works with the child.

For families who can afford it, private treatment is available through any of the professionals listed above.

Parents who struggle valiantly with problems they are unable to resolve usually feel very relieved when they do not have to carry the burden by themselves any longer. Therapy means the beginning of a healing process. It also means that they and their children can look forward to a normal happy life everybody has a right to enjoy.

BIBLIOGRAPHY

Books and Pamphlets for Adults

1001. Isaacs, Susan. *Troubles of Children and Parents.* New York: Schocken Books, 1973. (First published 1948.)

Contains a discussion on various symptoms of difficulty.

1002. Kellerman, Jonathan. *Helping the Fearful Child: A Guide to Everyday Problems and Anxieties.* New York: W. W. Norton, 1981.

Focuses on problems related to fears and anxieties. Provides a clear distinction between "normal" fears and those requiring professional help.

1003. Mayer, Greta, and Hoover, Mary. *When Children Need Special Help with Emotional Problems.* New York: Child Study Association of America, 1961.

This helpful pamphlet lists symptoms that may give reason for concern by age levels. Also includes resources for treatment.

1004. Shaw, Charles R. *When Your Child Needs Help: A Psychiatrist Looks at Emotional Problems of Children.* New York: William Morrow & Company, 1972.

Describes major childhood disorders in a nontechnical fashion. Includes causes, modes of diagnosis, treatment and outlook for the future.

1005. Spock, Benjamin. *Raising Children in a Difficult Time.* New York: Norton, 1974.

Commonsense discussion that should convince detractors that Dr. Spock is not at all "permissive." Helpful chapter on "Children Who Could Benefit from Psychotherapy."

AUTHOR INDEX

Numbers are item numbers

SUBJECT INDEX

Numbers denoting annotations are in italics

Adaptation. *See* Adjustment
Adjustment to school, 3–4,
  criteria for separation from mothers in, *61*
  effects of family stability in, 3–4, *66, 75*
  effects of past experience in, 3, 4, *58, 59, 60, 75, 596*
  factors in adaptation, 3, 4, *63*
  fathers' feelings in, *54*
  fears of children, *49, 62*
  feelings of children, *27*
  growth promoting experience as, 3–4, *50, 53, 55*
  infants and toddlers of. *See* Daycare for infants and toddlers
  information for parents, *26*
  need to remember mother's image. *See* Object constancy
  parent ambivalence in, 4, *13*
  phased, 3, 9, *50, 51*
  preparation for, *45, 56*
  readiness for, *16*
  recapitulation of developmental stages in, 3, 4, *61*
  regression in, 3, *61*
  after short absence, *23, 39*
  stages of development, effects of, *49*
  temperamental differences, effects of, *42*
  vulnerable periods for, 3, *33, 37*
  when new baby is born, *133*
Aggression, 178–179
  anxiety, due to, *203, 948*
  dealing with, *759, 762, 784, 949*
  see also School and preschool
  and emotional release, *772, 773, 784, 788, 863*
  fear due to, *203*
  and maturation, *884*
  permissiveness, due to, *808*
  preschool in. *See* School and preschool